Poems for the Heart and Mind

William E. Hardison

Poems for the Heart and Mind

Verses in a Homespun Style

TATE PUBLISHING
AND ENTERPRISES, LLC

Published by Tate Publishing & Enterprises, LLC
127 E. Trade Center Terrace | Mustang, Oklahoma 73064 USA
1.888.361.9473 | www.tatepublishing.com

Tate Publishing is committed to excellence in the publishing industry. The company reflects the philosophy established by the founders, based on Psalm 68:11,
"The Lord gave the word and great was the company of those who published it."

Book design copyright © 2013 by Tate Publishing, LLC. All rights reserved.
Cover art and design by William E. Hardison
Interior design and illustrations by William E. Hardison

Published in the United States of America

ISBN: 978-1-62902-926-9
1. Religion / Christian Life / General
2. Poetry / Subjects & Themes / Inspirational & Religious
13.11.07

Welcome friends. The contents are based strictly on the fibers and guidelines of high morality and goodwill, dedicated to all people whom believe and practice the good things in the eyes of our loving God and Savior. The primary intention of this author is to make a difference in the lives of the readers, by expressing here all the true joys, and agonies, while living and dealing with the "ups and downs" we all encounter, and hopefully fill a void with happiness. If this occurs with only one individual, then I'll feel my writings are not in vain.

Thanks, and May God Bless.

William E. Hardison

Dedication

In the name of the Lord, Jesus Christ,
whose spirit within me, instilled the strength and
attitude to express my thoughts of heart and mind.

Acknowledgment

To the memory of my Mom and Dad, for their tireless effort in good times, and in bad, to teach and live by the "golden rule."

Contents

Part 2:
Inspirations

Part 3:

Memories

Part 4:
Ideals

Part 6:
Troubled Waters

Part 7:
September Affair

PART 1:

HUMOR

Daily Food for Thought

Always look where you are
when driving in your car,
especially with a trooper on your tail;
for if you stare at him
through your rear-view mirror then;
you could be crashing through some fenced in rail.
Or, if you're talking on the phone
and in some far-off zone,
and the radio is playing a favorite theme,
then debris begins to fall
when you hit that concrete wall,
and they place you on a stretcher at the scene.
So keep your eyes alert
and you won't be "eating dirt,"
and you'll live to see another Christmas Eve;
but if you don't take heed,
you'll be sorrowful indeed;
'cause it may be other people you bereave.

To Spin Some Trends

Within my life I've often found
certain trends that come around;
for reasons that I don't know why.
Like it always seems it's Friday nights
when some nagging toothache strikes,
makes a grown-up want to cry.
'Cause all the dentists just flew down
to some convention out of town
on a big-time jet air bus;
and you're in pain o'er a three-day frame,
praying (for the dentists to return again,)
instead of cuss and fuss.
And the same thing happens
when you come down ill,
with need of an aspirin to instill,
and you lie at home by the telephone…
waiting for the doctor to come on.
But he's playing golf with his cell phone off,
while you suffer from the flu and cough.
So, once again it's a long weekend,
just dying for Monday to come again,
Well, it's just hard to comprehend!

Then comes time when it's hard to find
something that you lost before;
and you check each file, and search each pile,
until it becomes a bore;
but you count each one, one by one
'til your fingers and eyes are sore;
but you will find what you're looking for,
and it's always the last in store.
Now you'd think that the odds would blink,
and allow for just one time;

that the thing that's lost like an albatross,
would be the first to find.
Now here's a trend you may comprehend,
and one that I found out,
That when I plan a yard sale, and
it's been a long, long drought,
you can bet that the date I set,
it'll rain like hail…no doubt.

And I thought this through
and I have no clue;
but it's when I walk in grass,
and step into my dog's do-do…
hidden there where I pass.
And in one place with all that space
you'd think the odds aren't few;
that one footstep, is not a threat
for that to clog my shoe.
Now here is one about the rain and sun,
and it's when you wash your car;
on a sunny day you can wax away,
and it shines just like a star;
but it's oh so true when the job you do,
a storm comes blowing through.

Life's many trends…they have no ends;
and I can't submit them all,
but just this few I send to you,
to see if you agree;
for different folks have different strokes,
but it all seems true to me!

An Exodus

There's a place for family services
located in the mall;
with usual dental nervousness
by everyone who call.
Now the waiting room was crowded…
thirty seats, and all were full;
some people came for fillings,
while others, teeth to pull.

Now the dentist was extracting
on a patient in the chair,
when a noise came forth impacting
with a loud, unusual blare.
The sound was devastating
as it rattled through the wall,
it startled patients waiting,
even folks out in the mall.
The shrill of one huge drilling,
and the vibrant shook the place;
all heard the grind and grilling,
with a "look" on every face.
'Twas grinding like a motor
when a "burning" came about;
you could even smell the odor
that a drill-bit can put out.
Then was heard an awful screaming,
of someone bent in pain;
do you suppose the reaming
by the dentist was to blame?

Well, there came to be a finding
why that heavy noise occurred;
'twas found the drill and grinding,
by a (carpenter) was heard.
And somewhere in the drilling,
he slipped and went kaput.
The worker went a-spilling,
and the drill dropped on his foot.
Now can't you just imagine
that you're sitting in the lounge,
waiting for the dentist
for your time to come around?
When you hear that awful noise
of a drilling screeching out;
makes you wonder if for oil,
or in somebody's mouth.
Then, the office door swung open,
and (contented without doubt)
was the man who first went in,
and now is coming out.
But as he looked around,
not a single soul was there,
for all the patients in the lounge
had fled in total fear.

Back then as panic hovers,
I now confess it all,
I hauled tail with the others
to another dentist call.

The Marketers

There's a frenzy going on that many folks are prone;
when it comes to a weekend rummage sale.
They rise on Friday morn before the light is born
and head out on the bargain trail.
They park along the curb
with intentions to disturb,
'cause they hurry up to knock upon your door;
to rouse you out of bed
so they can get ahead,
to see the things you have in store.
They will even lend a hand to give their eyes a scan,
to help you put the junk out on the lawn.
They want to have a chance to get in that first glance,
to get the best of goodies and be gone.
So they'll swarm around your yard,
and places where they're barred,
like your attic, or the rest of your house;
but when you count your take,
no money did you make,
'cause all they did was browse.
Next, you got up Saturday morning
while the dark was still adorning,
all prepared to meet the rushing throng;
you're dressed and feeling swell before the daylight fell,
and you're all geared up to sell,
but not one single person came along.
So, that's the way it is when you deal with marketeers,
you really have to have it or you don't;
you can hoard junk year to year,
but if no values there appear,
well, they really don't know what they want.

The Old-Timer

While I was strolling down the street
one bright and sunny day,
skipping along with happy feet upon my merry way,
I came upon this gentle man rocking in his chair,
fanning with a makeshift fan to stir the humid air.
He looked to be 'bout ninety- three
with hair as white as snow,
and he cupped his eyes so he could see,
and his skin—was wrinkled so.
And he cupped his ear so he could
hear when I went up to speak,
and shook his hand when I got near,
and his grip was—oh—so weak.
I shouted then, "How are you friend,
could you share with me,
the secret to the life you spend, and your longevity?"
In a feeble way he starts to say: "This is how it is,
drink two to six packs of beer each
day along with six gin fizz.
And dance and dine with gals and wine,
and gamble through the night,
and do not stop to whine or pine…
keep on with all your might."
Then I said to him: "That's some great
trend, I think I'll try that too,
but do you mind, my old dear friend,
just how old are you?"
With an answer sly, and a wrinkled
eye, he said: "No, I don't mind,
I'm celebrating my birth today, I
just turned twenty-nine."

Only One Life to Live

One coffee for breakfast, one piece of toast,
one water with vitamin pill;
everything else I love the most
experts claim will kill.
For out of control, my cholesterol,
the clogging is doing me in;
They say this effect will take its toll
unless I begin this trend:
no omelets with cheese, with bacon, or ham,
no hominy grits or eggs.
No biscuits, no pork, no corned beef,
Spam, oh, how my hunger begs!
No butter, no bagels or waffles all hot,
or Dunkin' a sweet doughnut…
In a coffeepot with cream a lot, or
jam on my plate piled up.
But only one coffee, one toast, and
pill is breakfast that I take in,
and…this is supposed to last me until
I reach dinner, and then:
no mayonnaise, no crackers, no greasy french
fries, no roast beef, or any red meat,
No cookies or cakes or pizza pies, only one fish to eat.

No salt on the fish, no sweetening the
tea, no desserts, no peanuts, or beer.
"This hunger is taking its toll on
me, not cholesterol I fear."
No sauces or spices for 'tators that's hot,
just down 'em pure simple and plain;
"Will somebody pass me the dish I got? Oh! I'll never
go hungry again."
But only one 'tator, boiled fish—not
fried—is all of the dinner I ate.
At suppertime if I'm still alive, I'll
have this food on my plate:
One salad, one tea, which is sugar free,
and two slices of whole wheat bread;
If I don't go down with a clogged artery,
from starvation they'll find me dead!

Silly Senility

Memory has a funny way of fading to a blur,
many things remembered are not like they were.
I see a lot of faces from the past they will come,
without any name in mind to match with anyone.
And sometimes I watch some old movie show,
and oftentimes I see someone I think I know,
but cannot seem to place them in
that film made long ago.
Now, it was only yesterday while passing time away,
when someone met me in the mall—
whose name I couldn't say—
as we passed there in the hall.
Now, I couldn't place his face when he went by me
in haste- with nothing said at all!
And then I'm looking back to see
if he was looking back at me—
to see if I was looking back to see—
if he was looking back at me;
Well, it was as I thought it was, I thought it so because
he was thinking my same thought, and
looking back, brought pause!
I suppose it was the case he couldn't place my face,
so in our brain our memories strain;
maybe our paths will cross again,
and if they do I'll stop to greet, shake
his hand when we meet,
ask his name and then I'll see just
whose face was bugging me!

Back to School

Today's the day the kids return,
to some, the hour of gloom,
but others show a happy yearn
to fill their new class room.
But the happiest ones—I suspect,
are parents whom are glad,
for summer long the pool and deck
has worn out Mom and Dad!

The Penny Pincher

There is a well-known "saying"
which refers to all your "dough"—
that you cannot take it with you when you're
called upon to go!
And in this verbal "saying"
which has always proven true,
is your money will be staying
when your hearse delivers you.
Now there is a message sending
which is aimed at hoarding cash,
that your kinfolks will be spending
all the money that you stash.
So, don't be tight regarding
all this wealth that you possess,
for when it's time for parting,
you'll leave in happiness.
For life is short becoming,
just throw caution to the wind,
your heartstrings will be strumming
when you hang it out and spend.
'Cause riches aren't just everything
held tightly to the vest,
but much the "pain" that it can bring—
that misers can attest.
So, loosen up, untie your roll,
and enjoy your good health.
Cast away the lust for gold…
just go with what life dealt!

Over the Hill

If it ain't one thing, it's another,
with facts that daily unfold;
of trends that occur which I will refer
and mostly affecting the old.
Like bending to tie up the laces,
or to trim the toenails down,
but it's not the bending that hinders,
but the raising back up I've found.
It's the glaring of light that follows…
from blood that's draining the brain,
my eyes come stark with eyelids dark,
oh, I dread that bending again!
And it's so easy to long remember
events from decades in stow;
it's because I find we recall the time,
but forget things minutes ago.
And there's pain in my back from raking,
but it's now just starting to heal;
from massaging and heat I managed to treat,
now it's pain in my legs I feel.
And my sight grows dimmer and dimmer,
when in from sun and about;
and the glasses I wear for sun-lit glare,
I can't see with or without!
And tying a tie is horrendous,
my wife takes on this chore,
and buttons my shirt 'fore going to church
this lady I truly adore.
With grandkids growing much taller and lean,
come thoughts so sober and real;
that all these things that living now brings,
just proves I'm "over the hill"!

But I still cut grass and hedges I trim,
and change oil in two different cars,
and I do other deeds like pulling up weeds,
although I'm "seeing stars."
And I work in my garden with tiller and hoe,
to find more time to kill;
not bad for a man whose lifetime span
has put him "over the hill."
there's comfort in knowing the tough keep going,
although the going is tough;
an adage true that I always knew
would fill my need enough.
I've seen the woes in living long,
I've met the good and bad;
I've been through things that illness brings,
but I'm still here and I'm glad!
But not only glad but thankful too,
things could really be worse,
I could even be dead or laid down in bed
with having a full-time nurse.
And "over the hill" are just three words,
you're young as you may feel,
just bear the fain as Christ felt pain
if you are really ill.
To all my friends, both young and old,
I bid you all goodwill,
just stay the course and view the source,
when you get "over the hill!"

What's in a Name?

Now everybody all have names,
everything else does too;
so everyone should make their aims
to find out which and who!
It never fails I must confess
that when I'm waved upon,
it's always "hey" on their address,
or "hi there" on the phone.
For many years I wondered why
folks just wouldn't say…
my real true name which I rely,
instead of names like "hey."
Even now, when I hear "hi there"
I think they're calling me,
but then I guess it's better fare
than name of "do hickee."
There's "thing a ma jig" or "wha's his name,"
along with "thing of ma bob."
they're not intended to defame,
but ego it will rob!
There's also "ding-a-ling," "do lolly pop,"
"whatcha ma callit" or "do dad,"
"rink a dink" and "beepedy bop"
or other names I've had.
And here I add there is a trend
that some folks seem to show,
that even as a close-by friend,
my name they still don't know!
The most precious thing we have on earth
for with us mortals stay;
is our very name we got at birth,

for everyone to say.
So if it's asking not too much,
be a little more direct,
and use not labels or the such,
but true names we respect!

To Bear Knot

Now this is just a silly tale
I'm sure you will agree,
but if it makes you smile a spell,
then that sure pleases me!
It's only just a play on "pun,"
the dictionary shows.
It's only for a little fun,
and this is how it goes:

"It's very tough to teach a bear
how to tie a knot.
Although your hands may be bare,
the bear's paws are not.
Just bear in mind, the bear's paws
are full of furry hair;
this very reason is because…
he is a grizzly bear!
For him, the bear to tie this knot…
is more than he can bear,
because it's fingers he has not,
but claws to claw his lair.
Now, here you need to bear some hope
that the bear must bear in mind,
that to tie a knot with rope,
is not as good as twine.
To tie a knot with string won't cope,
the strands are just too fine.
So, you must always bear in mind
that your bare hands cannot:
tie any knots with fishing line
to catch a fish or not!

And be aware that the bear
cannot bear in mind,
that this is all you can bear
with line of any kind!
So, why bother any bear
with tying knots at all?
the bear does not really care,
and on you, the burdens fall!

Say What!

There's no such thing as "future,"
as calendars relate;
and the "past" is just a memory
of our ever-"present" state.
For all our conscious living…
is the here and now we see,
and no matter how you view it…
won't change these facts that be.
So, don't plan for "tomorrow"
what you can do "today,"
for it may bring you sorrow,
and rewards will never pay.
Because "today" is not "tomorrow"
as you viewed it "yesterday",
and mistakenly the "future"…
if you look at it that way!
For "today" is now the "present,"
since "yesterday" has passed;
proves "tomorrow" never comes,
that "today" is always cast!
So, ever this remember:
that the "future" and the "past,"
"yesterday," "tomorrow"…
are "todays" in which we grasp!

Shad, Anyone?

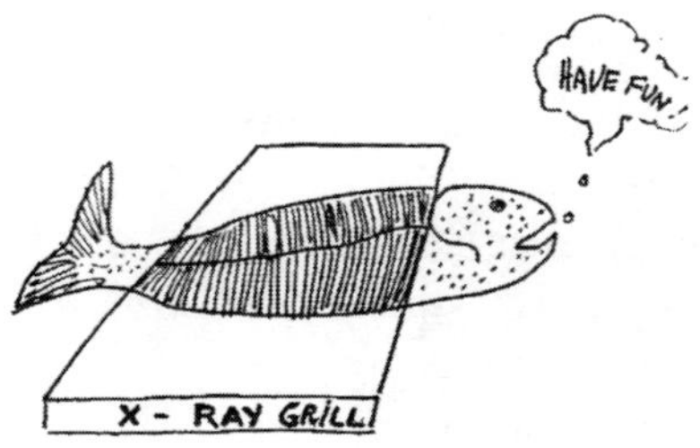

There's a gamely fish within the sea,
it's name is called a "Shad."
No better catch will ever be with all the fun you had!
There's always been a lot of say on how to cook this fish.
a bony "Shad" you can't fillet with all the bones of his.
To take this fish upon a dish and in the oven bake;
would be against a soundly wish…
for hours it would take!
To fry him in a frying pan would then be to quick;
The meat just wouldn't taste as good,
and too many bones to pick.
There is a mood with this seafood on
how to best prepare;
it's understood to take some wood
and make a plank with care;
the Shad you fix with spicy mix
and on that plank attach;
place on a grill, below you fill with
wood and fire a match.
Then roast that Shad until it's cured…
with ample time to cook;
for good results to be assured…
just give it one more look;
then with the plank where this Shad
lies, just swing it one big crank;
toss that fish far to the skies…
then eat that spicy plank!

The "Specs"

For those of you who aren't there yet
you're in for much surprise,
'cause as you age you'll need to get
some glasses for your eyes.
For twenty years I've had my share,
and they are one big pain,
not in my eyes, but you know where!
I'll try here to explain:
These "peepers" when I have them on
will fog and steam right up,
especially when I'm here at home…
from coffee in my cup;
or going out into the rains,
or working up a sweat;
moisture brings the biggest pains
that I've encountered yet.

And still there's other problems here…
like when they're in their case,
because they're always lost somewhere
when not upon my face!
Or when I bend to tie my shoes…
they always quickly fall…
upon the floor to get abused,
to break the frames and all.

And there were times I oft forgot
and left them in the car,
then look for days around the lot
just wondering where they are.
But after all they're what I need,
I'll try hard not to pout,
'cause with these specs I need to read;
as someday you'll find out!

Always Change

When you go to shop around,
you'll see upon the signs;
very clever prices bound
that always ends with nines.
From zero-nine to ninety-nine,
the cost is so arranged;
that what it means is what it deems;
that pennies are your change!
This is a trend I wish would end,
the one that deals with "change,"
the copper kind that builds with time,
and yet, no value claims.
A special change the "feds" should make
is do away with pennies;
for everybody's gracious sake

the pennies must diminish!
If all the pennies in the mint
were melted into pipes,
it would save the trouble spent,
the headaches and the gripes!
For pennies often load us down;
our pockets always fill;
they're everywhere they can be found,
'cause everywhere they spill.
They come and go in overflow
in every cup and jar,
down in a vase, in some suitcase
and floorboard of your car.
In pocketbooks or dining nooks,
the sofa and your chairs,
in all ash trays, in window bays,
and even on the stairs.
On tabletops, not-mentioned spots,
these pennies all have lain,
and they will stay in all our way
until this trend has waned.
It would suffice and be real nice
to round things to a dollar,
'Twould be no "change" to tax our brains
and be the trend to follow!

The Jack-Leg Carpenter

I love to build and hammer nails,
use level, square, and saw,
but in my work there seems to lurk a never-ending flaw;
that in my chores there often scores
some facts that brings a tear,
and turns into a mystery when pencils disappear!
I search beneath each block of wood,
each tool that lies around;
I sift the sawdust really good, but pencil can't be found.
I bring at least three or four to
make sure there's enough,
but should have brought about five
more to make the job less tough.

But when I build I'm all a-thrilled,
my ego's miles up high,
for all those pencils that I spilled,
I'll find them by and by.
And on the job there seems to lurk…a
trend to misplace things,
'cause I'm so excited in my work,
my pencils all "take wings!"
But oftentimes when on the look,
the answer will come clear;
that after searching every nook, I find one on my ear!

I'm just a jack-leg carpenter and thrive at what I do;
but complications do occur while working up a stew;
but end results are always found,
the best that I can claim,

and when I strow my tools around,
sometimes it brings me pain;
it's not just pencils that I lose, which brings me agony,
but it's the hammer that I use that gets the best of me!
It's the worst of any tool which finds a place to hide;
it makes me out a bumbling fool
when searching every side.
The hammer's so elusive when I lay it down a lot,
and the problem gets abusive when I lay it up on top:
of the high rung of my ladder that
I move around the shed,
and nothing comes more sadder when
that hammer hits my head!
It's not the way to find it there, up
where the thing has lain,
especially when it parts your hair
and causes all the pain.

Now, one would think a guy would
learn to keep it on his side,
and be a jack-leg's main concern
to keep his eyes real wide;
and try to keep things organized, if he intends to build;
and do it all in safety wise, instead of getting killed!

Out of Control

I have a little hand control that goes to my TV,
and somewhere in this wide-wide
world, it surely has to be.
For every time I put it down it seems to disappear,
and tho' I know it isn't so, it flees right in thin air!
I know it has no legs to walk, nor eyes to see and hide,
but every time I lay it down right there beside my side;
it finds a way to steal away before my very eyes;
and I look around, it can't be found, all logic it defies.

I've even tried to tie a string around my neck to hold
that testy, small evasive thing, so it can be controlled!
But often then for reasons thin it seems to get away,
and why it's so I just don't know,
and it goes on every day.
But it's been found in many spots, I'll just name a few:
My recliner pouch, beneath our
couch, under its pillows too.

On the floor, behind a door, and under Grandpa's clock;
In our bookcase, down in a vase,
and even a kitchen crock!

Down in the seat or in the pleat of my recliner chair,
the mantle there, upon a stair, or
beneath my dayroom cot;
or the sofa's lower flair.
The TV top, the fridge a lot (where it's often found!)
And I need that thing for me to bring
sanity to the sound (and to the sight as well!).

Is It Terminal?

It's the worst disease that's known to man
that experts came to know:
it grips someone like no ill can,
and makes a person slow.
With gender all it knows no bounds,
just rots away their soul.
It shies away their peers around,
as illness takes it toll.
It affects all people on this earth,
and bleeds away their pride.
It robs them of their inner mirth
where symptoms often hide.
The cure outlook for this disease
remains a little hazy,
but ease is best when victim sees;
their ailment is they're lazy.

Number 1

There is a strange phenomenon
that happens all the time;
and just what really brings it on
has always bugged my mind.
It's when I turn the water on
to wash my face and hands;
my kidneys start to act upon
in what the urge demands.
Or when I'm shopping in the mall
or driving down some street,
I best not see a waterfall
or fountain that I meet.
I've often thought if other ones
have known this to be so,
that just because some water runs—
it makes them want to go!
But, this is life and what it brings;
the least of what befalls,
for I must live with tougher things,
not just when nature calls!

The Dove

It happened this past Easter
at a crowded city church,
where many came to worship
for their souls there to search.
And in that congregation
sat some "highfalutin" ones,
whom came to show their garments off
whenever Easter comes.
Now in the eyes of others
you don't know how you look,
'til you have awareness that…
"you've had your picture took!"
For sitting in the mass
was a lady all agleam,
with her bluish, blackish lashes,
and her rosy facial cream.
There she sat so "high and mighty"
just peering all around…
as if the Lord had sent her

in a frilly bonnet crown;
to captivate an audience
with performance "Ala Grand,"
and send them home believing
she's the queen of wonderland.
But wait! There's something on it,
when you take the time to stop,
to see upon her bonnet
a whiteish, grayish spot,
It's a sight that's not becoming
to a person "dressed in style,"
who's so busy there exploiting
a broad fictitious smile.
Now it seem the only answer
comes from heaven up above,
where a sign of revelation came;
by droppings from a dove!

To Meet My Call

My family calls me Billy,
but my friends all call me Bill.
My teachers called me Willie
and my preacher calls me Will.
My wife, she calls me William
and the Doc calls when I'm ill.
Now my middle name is Edward
so my coach, he called me Ed.
And some have called me Eddie,
but Edward, some have said,
but they can call me anything…
just call in time for bed!
Some folks have called me "Hardy"
for last name, Hardison,
and many times they tagged me:
"that old son of a gun."
But they can call me any name
as long as it's in fun.
But names I'm called a-plenty
and I'll just list a few,
because it's just too many
to cite here unto you.
One of those is "dummy"
while another one is "smart,"
many call me "funny"
and some may say "old fart"
And folks have called me "stingy"
another word is "tight."
"Curve Ball" was heard a-plenty…
(my baseball pitch in flight.)
I'm labeled as "lock bowel"
"lock washer" or just "lock"

"A charming wise old Owl,"
or "a head as hard as rock."
More names like "nerd" and "bird"
and you may add "Jackass,"
"absurd" is one I've heard…
along with "he's a gas."
But they can call me anything,
as long as it's for cash!
Been called at home by telephone
by busy marketeers.
Was called to work by railroad clerk
for many a night or day,
but they can call me anytime
as long as it's for pay!
I'm sometimes called a "croaker"
and often called a "dunce,"
many times a "joker"
when buddies come to bunch,
but they can call me anything,
as long as it's for lunch!

The Gizmo

There has to be a "gizmo" thing
upon my auto hood,
some sort of tool invisible,
and not one understood.
I've often tried to locate it,
but much to no avail,
still there it sights the traffic lights,
and never known to fail.
For when I drive in traffic's flow…
in days and even nights,
it always seems to change the beams
as I approach those lights.
The strangest thing that "Gizmo" brings,
is it always turns 'em red;
and I've never seen it turn 'em green,
it's always red instead!
So in my woe I watch the glow
of every "red" in town,
but on I drive and I will strive
to keep my temper down.
Tho' see him not, he's in a spot…
in case there is a wreck,
this thing, "Gizmo," is first to go,
and breaks his little neck!

Joe, Jo, Bo, Bow, and Arrow

Now there was Bo and girlfriend, Jo,
whom he loves so dear;
and Jo calls Bo her handsome beau,
and Bo is Jo's hero.
Bo ask Jo if she would go…
to hunt with Bo for deer,
Bo asks Joe, a pal of Bo,
to come along sincere.
So there goes Jo, Bo, and Joe…
to hunt with bow for deer,
they all shoot the bow and arrow,
a sport they love so dear.
Then Jo and Bo, but not pal Joe,
they both spot a deer;
Bo fired the arrow from his bow
and missed by ten feet clear!
Jo told Joe and Bo to get down low…
when she took her shot to go;
and while she missed the fleeing doe,
Jo shot her beau, poor Bo!

Where's the Beef

We chimed in festive mood
while waiting for our food…
in a restaurant of jolly song and cheer;
and all around they sat,
our friends in usual chat,
while aroma from the kitchen filled the air.
There were many tables there,
but only one was bare,
and of course that happened to be ours;
some had ordered steak, while some had fish to bake,
by now the time grew into hours.
And we could hardly wait,
for the time was growing late;
I even heard someone's tummy growl;
and as we looked around and saw others
gulping down,
that's when we began to holler foul!
Now with our fork and spoon,
our swoon turns into gloom,
and we're stricken down in disbelief;
for what the waiter brought,
the precious food we sought,
I heard someone cry out: " Where on earth's the beef?"
For that puny thing I saw
was a piece of something raw,
with a little bit of rice to top it off;
but 'twas good to be with friends
and the pleasure that it sends,
something that forever can't be bought!

PART 2:

INSPIRATIONS

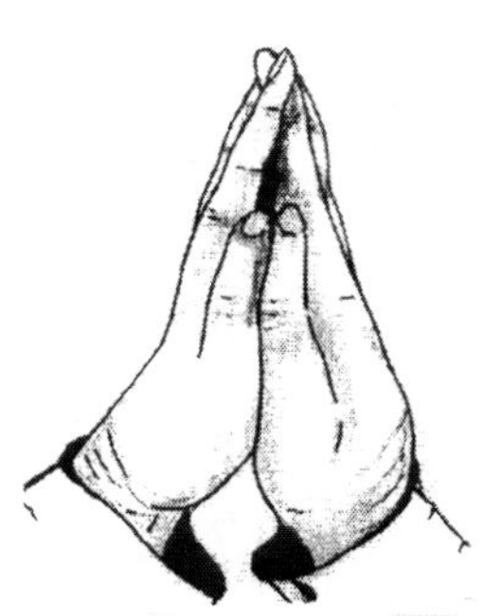

Best Choice

We wake up every morning,
and we go to bed each night.
We spend each day performing
a thing that's wrong or right.

But do we stop to think
just what our choices are?
Do we ever reach the brink
of having gone too far?

Do we ever realize
a better way to go?
To do the things that satisfies
to give our lives more glow!
There are two choices in our lives,
the first, and best I know;
is holding on to Jesus Christ,
the next, is let Him go.
So, I suggest you cling to Him,
as He, upon the cross,
bearing all the brunt of sin,
and pain at any cost.

But If you choose to let Him go,
your life will always be;
an empty thing that struggles so,
and ends in misery.

But take the Lord within your breast,
accept Him as your own;
your very soul will come to rest
with Jesus on the throne!

The River of Life

Over this river of life we flow,
Down the currents sail,
Upon the changing tides we go…
Fighting tooth and nail.
It is a long and rocky route
For all us sailors be;
Some souls will reach their goals throughout,
While some are lost at sea!
We're traveling with a hope for peace,
Of love, and harmony;
And striving for all wars to cease…
'Til everyone is free!
So we're sailing on this river of life
To some far better place;
Where absent are the woes and strife,
Just dwell in God's embrace!

The Handwriting
on the Wall

There's a slogan often used
by folks who get confused,
referring to a vision they can see;
no, it's not a "crystal ball"…
but, "handwriting on the wall,"
it's true, because it just occurred to me!

I had found myself subdued
in a dreary, pensive mood,
caught up in a melancholy way;
I was lonely and depressed,
restless with unrest,
and my troubled heart was filled with dismay.
And from distant times it comes;
the memory of loved ones,
family members whom have passed;
and then I came aware
there's no friends around who care,
just added to the shadow that was cast.

Tho' in the comfort of my home,
I felt so all alone,
as I wallowed in self pity I declared;
and I thought about my youth,
too young to know the truth…
about the woes of strife that lay ahead;
like the fears of growing old
from the years that take a toll,
and thinking of the things that shouldn't be;
but now I realize

that right before my eyes,
a vision of that slogan comes to me:

"You're not alone at all"
said the writing on the wall,
"you have the best there is with much to spare,
you have Dear God above…
Who showers you with love,
and all your heavy burdens He will bear.
There is Jesus to abide,
and your wife is by your side,
with siblings and your kinfolks to confide.
And with many people blind,
while others are confined,
should make your silly feelings all subside.
A lovely home in place,
a life you dare not waste,
children and grandchildren in the fold,
so you need not be afraid
for Christ will surely aid,
He's the best friend you have…to save your soul."
This brought me to my feet,
with a thought of great relief,
for now I know I've seen it all,
and no matter who you be,
you too, may come to see:
a writing you believe is on the wall!

Nowhere to Hide

There is an old saying among us,
one that is often denied;
but the truth of the adage still lingers:
"you can run, but you never can hide."
Way "down in the dumps" may find us
when sorrow has taken its toll;
but seeking a haven of comfort,
we ran instead of console.
When fear and despair are the demons…
that offer most wretched of rides,
robbing our precious freedoms
that God has so well supplied.
"Grab life by the horns" and hold it,
with Jesus, our savior, and guide;
leading us to salvation,
and never to run or hide.
The world is evermore turning,
'twas meant for spinning aloft;
not stopping for some forlorn loser,
to let this somebody off!
Facing this life is so awesome,
just fill it with gladness and pride,
turning to God, for He loves us,
'cause we'll never get out…alive!

The Master Architect

God is the master architect
who surveyed all the world…
with wonders grand He drew a plan
for creation to unfurl.
He formed the world with powers great,
and after this was done;
He build the skies for light to rise…
for this He made the sun!
And in the beauty of the night
His wonders now unveil;
the full moon bright with silver light
and stars that cast their spell.
His splendid touch of master art
brought forth the mighty earth;
He then proceeds to sow the seeds
that gave all nature birth.

And as the master architect,
He structured each and all;
with greatest ease He formed the seas
and carved the mountains tall!

He planted all the woodlands free,
with many loving things,
and it is here where we can hear
the songs that nature sings!
He cut away the earthly clay
to meet the river's flow;
and filled these streams with sunlit gleams
to make the waters glow.

He is the greatest architect
and here's His fondest dream;
to top His plan, creating man
and finish up His scheme…
with one last chore He had in store,
and this completely done;
to give to us the one we trust,
Lord Jesus Christ His Son!

The Last Flight Home

My appetite is on the soar,
I cannot get enough,
but it's not the food
I'm craving for…
but life to fill me up!
My great desire for living so…
is hunger on a spree,
this love for life from head to toe is churning
within me.
For long I met each coming day
and never gave much thought;
to all the years that's given way,
and aging that they brought.
But, Father Time has made aware
that life is short indeed;
with mother nature's love affair…
just fits the mould I need.
To see the morning sun-lit
gleams across the dew-filled grass,
and breathe the freshness that it brings,
will always with me last.
Or view the sunset's crimson glow
that creeps below the shore…
to cast a colorful rainbow,
makes my heart yearn for more!
Or on some bright-lit starry night
when all is quiet and still,
I dream about that special flight
that only dreamers feel.
To have a friend drop by awhile
and "chew the fat" or so,
or see a neighbor wave and smile,

are best things that I know.
Except for one, that's heaven's home,
the best plan in God's sight;
for time has come for this old one
to plan his final flight.
The journey to eternal life,
through happiness and prayer;
free in Christ and free from strife,
a cross I yearn to bear.
So here on out,
no fear or doubt will take me by the hand,
only God, and heaven's route leads
to that promised land!
There's so much more that I can say,
I just don't have the time;
too many things that come my way
that fills my heart and mind.
But, I hope you get the meaning here;
this message I suggest: you too,
can lose your doubt and fear,
by God's pure simple test:
Is make amends for all your sins
in name of Jesus Christ,
take your troubles all to Him…
will get you on that flight!

The Master Artist

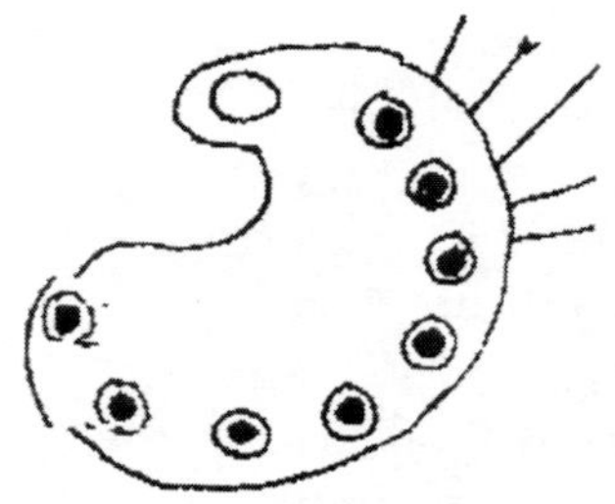

There is a Master Artist,
the greatest of them all;
Who painted the canyons
and the mountains tall;
Who painted the crimson
in the sunset's glow,
then captured the brilliance
in a great rainbow!
He mixed up purple
for the morning dawn,
Vandyke brown
for the yearling fawn.
He painted in the green
of the whispering pines,
then brushed in their needles
with masterful lines.
He sketched in the oceans
that run so deep,
then painted them with motions
that forever keep.
He shaded in the shadows
in the river's flow,
and painted green fields

where sweet flowers grow.
He painted the sky
with bright Prussian blue,
then put in the clouds
with their silver hue.
And then in black
came the dark midnight,
but also the shine
of the bright moonlight.
Then came Jupiter,
Pluto and Mars,
and He rounded out the universe
with twinkling stars.
Now His masterpiece is finished
with a wonderful glow,
and the Artist smiles from heaven,
His studio!

How Firm Is Your Foundation?

Take any building-structure, in range from short to tall,
and having many sizes from huge to very small;
they have one thing in common—a
low-foundation wall.
Although it may look solid, some weakness may exist,
brought on by many factors that arises in its midst,
and as you view that building, you may not see its list.
So, as you look upon it, it may not be as well
as the sight that you are seeing,
since you could never tell
that in that mighty body, weak foundations dwell.
Thus, the building is no stronger than
the blocks it's resting on,
and the footing is no greater than the
ground that spreads beyond.
With a weak foundation never…
does a body stand alone!
Now, man is like that structure with little to rely,
His footing wroth with weakness,
but nothing looks awry.
His body's strong appearance deceives the human eye.
Thus, man is no more stronger than
beliefs he's resting on,
and his steps are no more truer than
the ground he treads upon,
and his footing is no surer than his will to overcome!
How firm is your foundation? Does
your standing list or sway?
Are your footsteps planted squarely
upon this earthly clay?
Do you stand on your convictions?
Are you solid when you pray?

If you, your body's structure, meets that building code,
then all the strength it musters—never will erode,
then all your life's endeavors can haul the heavy load!
So, when your time has passed and
you've met it's every test;
you've strengthen every column where
upon your structures rest,
You have met your builder maker,
you have done your very best!

The Wall

Be not weary of it friend;
about life's woeful bout;
there are things that enter in
that you can do without!
Hard times come and hard times go;
just hold your head up high,
and hang in there and take the blow;
that's where your strength will lie.
In these times of fear and doubt,
when life deals you a spin,
just chew it up and spit it out
and take it on the chin!
But you may say in your dismay:
"there's too much to deny;
the many things that come my way…
that seem to go awry."
The answer lies in God above,
He'll show you what to see—
the beauty of the things you love,
and let the others be.
Blind or sight He gives you light
to view His wonders true;
The warm sunshine, the feel of night,
the freshness of the dew.
A breath of life, an appetite,
a chance to walk and talk,
a heart to beat for whom you meet,
a choice you must not balk.
And focus on your house and home,
your family and kin,
everything that's good to own
brings happiness within.

And best of all on God you call,
He'll take away your plight,
and Jesus Christ will be your wall
to bar away the strife.

One Cross for All

Have mercy, Lord, my precious Lord,
I pray not just for me;
but other ones whose hurting comes,
are worse than mine can be.
No matter how I suffer here
with all my aches and pain;
some other's ills are rougher still
on this old misery lane.
But it's a path we all may tread
to deal with vicious woe,
the many things that illness brings,
that living has in stow.
For I've seen the smiling faces shine
of those who walk with pain,
of many found with braces bound,
and some who live in vain,
those, whose limbs are paralyzed,
and folks who cannot see,
they offer me—a token free,
responding happily.
And I feel my own ill dwindle down
as their courage reaches me;
for in my heart a flame they start
turns all my thoughts to Thee;
For You're the One who suffered most
through all Your love and care;
it's our remorse beneath the cross,
of pain You had to bear!

My Pilot

In daily grind, sometimes I find an urge to steal away,
to some lone spot, a peaceful lot, when I am in dismay.
So off I trot to that quiet spot, a forest stream or creek,
where nature dines and beauty
shines are company I seek!
Where wildlife croons their gleeful
tunes in their own paradise…
God's scheme of things which clearly
brings the wonders He applies.
Now resting here I sense Him near,
His presence fills the air;
He's in the trees, He's in the leaves,
the stream, He's everywhere!
From mid the creek I hear Him speak
in voice of rippling waves;
He's there in sight as geese take flight,
a scene my memory saves.
While here I gaze through evening's
haze in show of sunset's glow.
I see the leaves from trees fall free
and drift on with the flow.
I see God's plan in thoughts I scan
that man is like those leaves;
Who lives and dies before God's eyes
in life that God so weaves,
then on some river just drift forever
in beauty of nature's realm;
where one can say "No More Dismay"
with God there at the helm!

A Greater Force

There is no power here on earth
Can match the one above.
There is no force that's given birth
Can win as much as love.
Of all the mighty guns of war,
None have gained a friend,
But all the care of friends that are,
Brings strength that comes within.
It is the hand of God that rules
In spite of what men say.
It is the greed that make men fools
And leads them all astray.
And blood may flow along the way
By some misguided deed,
And one may choose to live each day
Without a care to heed.
But in the end he'll surely fall
With all his thoughts to deem,
For when he comes to gain his pall,
'Tis God, his judge supreme.

The Path

In this world so ill afflicted—
Winds a path o'er rocky ground;
Treading through the thorn and thicket,
Heading onward, homeward bound.
Tho' the route be long and weary,
Stop we often there to pray;
Be the journey ever dreary,
God will guide us on our way.
Through the fog and mist there resting—
With a trail so scantly seen,
All our faith is put to testing—
By dear God who reigns supreme.
So, when the road has reached an ending,
Where we meet the one we love,
Then we've carved a path ascending
To our Father up above!

The Master's Plan

God has a plan that never fails,
It's one that guides us all
Through many times of dreary spells
And lifts us should we fall.
And fall we will if footsteps tread
Down life's lone rocky trail;
Forgetting how Christ's blood was shed
And pain that He befell.
Forgetting that He braved the cross
To save our souls from hell…
To see His cause as just a loss
And not our Father's will.
But in the Master's scheme of things
God wants the world to see:
That Jesus Christ, the King of kings,
Is hope for you and me.
That we must act upon His plan
By every sin confess,
And bonding with our fellow man
Will bring us happiness.
By holding trust and faith in Him;
To glorify His name…
And show compassion to all men
Will satisfy His aim.
And last, not least, is loyalty
With will to understand:
That having faith in God's decree…
Will guarantee His plan!

An Active Member

I'd like to think as time goes by
that I'm the lucky one;
that I received my piece of pie
and my place in the sun;
that I stood tall and met my call
and lived life's full demand;
by doing right to each and all
with trust and helping hand.
That I was there in their despair
to comfort or console—
to ease the pain they came to bear
when miseries unfold.
Now I'm no saint nor preacher man,
but have my own desires,
to have a will to build good will,
to do what God inspires.
And I believe I pay my dues
for life's both joy and woe.
Each day I live I try to choose
the best ways that I know,
but in our chain of life we find
a missing link or two;
it may have been some fault of mine
or maybe one by you,
but either way I'm bound to try,
to dedicate my best,
to do what's right by God on high,
and He will do the rest!

The Lost Lamb

I bow my head in shame, dear Lord
for long neglecting thee;
I had been living by the sword,
but still, You stayed by me.

I knew that You were always there,
and yet, I turned an eye;
and many times I felt despair
though You were there close by.

I searched for strength another way
down life's deep darker lane,
and this poor lamb who went astray,
has come to know the pain.

Please bring me back into the fold,
beneath Your guiding hand,
oh Lord, my life has been so cold,
I need Your warmth again!

So now I bow my head and pray
and humbly beg of Thee,
to ask forgiveness for the way
I failed You selfishly.

Now in my heart I hope and feel
Your holy presence dear,
and in my life a void has filled;
since now that You are here!

The Best Side

Whatever we plot from bottom to top,
and whether it helps us or no,
we're on a path of eternal wrath
of strife in a world of woe.

Some wallow each day in hollow dismay,
and never they stop to pray,
but praying they don't, it's trouble they want,
and problems will stay that way!

So to each his own, whether young or grown,
each one has a life to hone;
and try they must to pry out the lust
of evil that many are prone.

Now here's a side that all should abide,
and that is to goodness subscribe,
to gain all the strength of a heavenly saint
and in God's work confide.

So, let's all pitch in and cast away sin,
and with a new life begin;
for at judgment date at the pearly gates,
our friend Jesus will lead us within!

Takes Only One Blessing

When evening shadows come to fall
at close of weary days,
just count your many blessings all,
not sorrows or dismays.
For oftentimes we dwell on woes,
and often we forget;
that even tho' ill winds may blow,
means not our end is met.
For God has given us our gifts,
our lives, for which we owe
our soul to Him for which He lifts
when hard times come to tow.
And every blessing that we count,
even if it's one,
just a simple, honest, small amount,
God sees it as a ton!

Time After Time

My, oh my, how time does fly,
like winds from a hurricane,
swiftly blown to the vast good-bye…
as smoke does from a flame!

And the days and weeks like a bullet streaks
to the past with lighting speed…
to find some mark where dreams embark,
to fill a dreamers need.

And the months and years like javelin spears
just soar past overhead…
to reach some goal where the weak and bold…
meet up with the lives they led.

But in meanwhile just hope and smile,
and count your blessings all;
for near the end you can depend
on God, to whom we call!

Sinking Sand

We're treading on this road of life
enclosed by "sinking sand."
Winding up and down and all around
to reach that promised land.
It's up to us to keep our trust;
to do what God demands;
to go the way without astray
into those "sinking sands."
For once in there, the Devil's lair,
we'll sink with endless pain;
unless we change and find the range
to straight our sights again.
It's not just footprints in the sand
we want the world to find;
but those that's found on solid ground
are ones you leave behind.
So, steer the course with much remorse
and focus on our goals;
where faith expands, so "sinking sands"
will never claim our souls!

Beyond the Sea

There is a magical stairway
that spirals up through the sky;
it winds its way where angels stay
to mighty God on high!

Across the mystic sea I view
each step a golden glare;
far into a world of blue,
I long to make it there;
to yond horizon's secret realm
my yearning heart explores;
like captains at their guiding helm
in search for safer shores.
Where, God upon the throne He rests
with Jesus by His side;
where I'll receive eternal bliss
that only they provide.
So there beyond the ocean's roar,
this gateway beckons me…

up to heaven's open door
where every soul is free.

The trail is rocky I surmise,
but I shall carry on...
until I reach my paradise,
my everlasting home!

The Man Upstairs

With hope and cares for the Man Upstairs…
I search for His guiding light.
I yearn with a will for my heart to fill
for a need in my earthly plight.

I have no gold, but a hungry soul,
which is wealth of my whole affairs;
It's the gift He gave and the one He saved…
by the grace of the Man Upstairs.

And the Man Upstairs with our souls He spares
if we follow His master plan;
is believe in Him and confess our sin,
and be kind to our fellow man.

And look to Him when our lives grow dim;
to His wonders that never cease;
and when in doubt throw the Devil out,
assuring us lasting peace.

Now the days go by and my time draws nigh,
and nothing I see compares:
to the blessed love and the cares above,
coming from the Man Upstairs!

My Own Grist Mill

There is a wheel of life in me
that turns my ills away.
It grinds away the strife I see
that comes with every day.

It churns along with love and hope,
the meal within my soul;
it creates chance to live and cope
with troubles that unfold.

This wheel of life I lubricate
with God's own precious words;
which clears away all sin and hate,
the grime that oft occurs.

I keep it spinning day and night
to keep my bearings straight…
around the axle of my life…
to reach my judgment date!

Seven Days Without God Makes One Weak

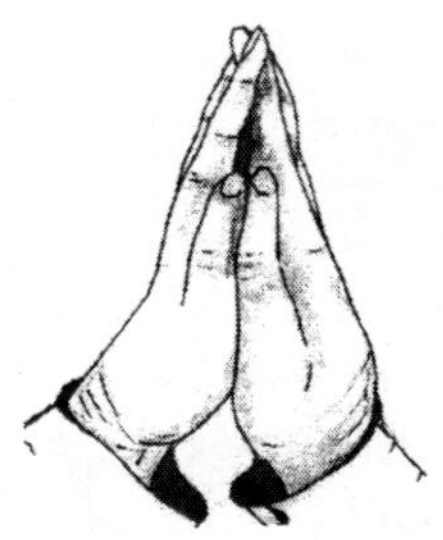

Do you feel downtrodden
And sad with emptiness?
Or that you've been forgotten
And your life is in a mess?

Has your mind been so annoyed
That this has made you weak?
Do you need to fill this void,
But you have no clues to seek?

For these questions that I'm posing,
There's something you can do;
It will lead you to eroding
The ills affecting you.

The answer is to follow
With a very strong belief,
That every day that's hollow,
Have a will to deal with grief:

Just start each day with Monday
And pray with all your might,
And when you reach next Sunday,
Your goal should be in sight;
For on that day surrender
Every ill that you possess,
And God is there so tender
To take them from your breast!

God Is Watching Us

God is watching us from heaven's way
and sees us one and all;
in everyway of come what may,
He's there to catch our fall.

To tread a straight and righteous path,
it should behoove us all;
to fear God's wrath, a mighty craft,
but heed His loving call.

God is watching while we're sleeping,
and watches when we rise,
comforts us when weeping
if we should meet demise.

He's by us while we're on the job
to keep us safe and warm;
for while at work if dangers lurk,
He'll shelters us from harm.

He's the light that takes the darkness out,
adds hope for all despaired;
calms the doubts of all with bouts
of many folks impaired.

God is watching us and counting names
and keeping records too;
His very aim is "Staking Claims"
for those who make it through.

So, lift your eyes to God on high,
return His lasting care,
and by and by you'll see Him nigh…
amid the trumpet's blare.

But cast your sight down to the ground,
and shun dear God above,
the Devil's pound will drag you down…
to Satan's fiery cove!

Open Up

Surrender all your lives to God,
allow His spirit in;
and every path you choose to trod
will lead away from sin.

So let Jesus be a friend indeed,
dear Christ, God's only Son,
He'll satisfy your every need
from now to kingdom come!

Now open up your minds and hearts
to His eternal care,
and all the blessings He imparts
will come to us in prayer!

Our Way

There's a need for inspiration, a daily revelation,
something that will guide us on our way…
to destiny and love; to our heaven up above,
where everyone will meet some sweet day.

And the hour is getting late, and many cannot wait
to meet their Mighty Maker in the sky;
Surely time will come as does the setting sun,
we'll see our loving savior by and by.

In all our future pain it will never be in vain;
for our Lord has taken care of that;
for He suffered on the cross so there would be no loss,
so every single soul could adapt.

Now upon each precious hour do not hide in cower,
simply rectify to God and pray;
This is the best solution to relieve the much confusion,
and clear the many objects in our way.

Because our goal is heaven,
we count each day to seven,
on each, we have a duty to fulfill;
To love our God and neighbors, to
stay in their good favors,
and to all endearing friends show goodwill!

The Book

There is a great day coming soon,
and in glory's path I wait;
I feel the thrill of the trumpet's tune
in rapture of my fate.

I hear the roll of the drummer's snare,
an aurora gleams on high;
I feel God's presence everywhere
as judgment day draws nigh.

And He will come as once before,
but this time in His hands,
He'll hold the names He has in store
within the book of lambs.

And listed there are faithful ones,
all those God chose to sign.
For faithful souls is why He comes,
and one of them is mine!

In His Hands

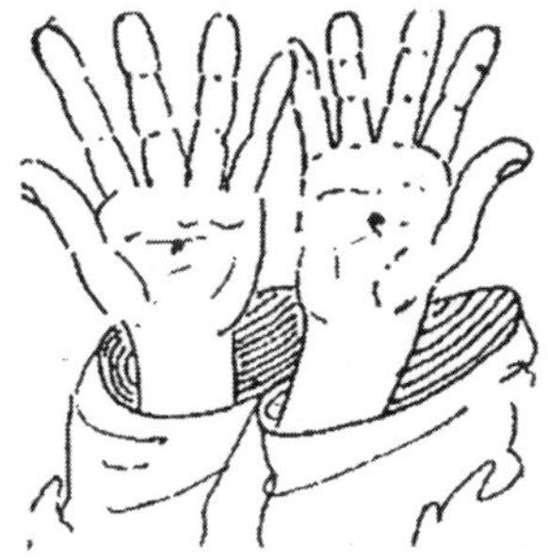

I chill as distant thunder roars,
and see the lightning sky,
a spirit deep within me soars
that God is drawing nigh!

I feel His storm within my veins,
and feel its rushing flow;
the very force in which He reigns;
that everyone should know.

The awesome wrath of God prevails
within His mighty hands.
As raging winds of awesome gales
for whom needs reprimands.

"But do not fear the storm, I say…
but God to whom you bow,
to fear Him, love Him and obey
will bring our finest hour."

So through the storm, it's love to seek,
respect His hands of wrath,
for fearing God is not seen weak,
but strength on glory's path!

Rendezvous

Oh, how wonderful the scene,
so vivid and serene
when I view my rendezvous
with God on high.

And how powerful I find
this dream upon my mind,
and this yearning in my bosom will not die!

Yes, the meeting will be great
when I reach the pearly gates,
leaving worldly trophies far behind;
where my Savior's arms will hold
my trusting, loving soul,
and the paradise of heaven will be mine.

So in the very end
I'll meet my dearest friend,
Jesus Christ who led me through the years.
He always held me up,
He always "filled my cup,"
and always brought me joy
and calmed my fears.

I passed not every test,
but held Him to my breast
'til the vicious winds of turmoil would subside.
And after all is said and done
I've relied on God's true Son,
Jesus Christ, the Savior
is my guide!

Tho' this world I'll be so leaving,
show no weeping or no grieving,
a simple *adios* will give suffice.
For I gave it all I had
in good times and in bad,
and rewards pay much greater
in God's own paradise!

My Savior Lives Within Me

My Savior lives within my life,
pure sacred and so dear,
I yearn for heaven's paradise…
that brings me comfort here.
I rise up when the morning calls
with Jesus on my mind;
and when the evening darkness falls,
He's made my day sublime!
Dear Jesus has complete control
as time goes marching by,
the very thought He owns my soul
will keep my spirits high.
And in my heart I'll hold Him there
from now to glory be,
for all my troubles He will bear
from here…eternally!

A Bit of a Lift

Poetry is the spice of life that lifts a soul in need.
When strife has cut you like a knife,
A poem is what you read.

Your brain is like a set of wires
That takes the best of care.
To read a poem your heart inspires—
Eliminates repair.

So, if your faith and hope expires,
Just read some soothing ode,
And sweet desires run through those wires
To ease the heavy load.

How restful are those words of prose
That conquer ills in stow;
To banish strain and all your woe—
Read Edgar Allan Poe!

So, keep your wires connected right,
For all have roles to play,
Each one a route to something bright,
And not to sad dismay.

Just stack a pile of poems up,
The prose and those in rhyme,
Then read 'em all and "fill your cup",
It's so much worth your time!

Home at Last

I know it's true
without ado,
from heaven God will call;
if I believe and I concede
that Jesus died for all.

God will forgive
when I relive
and act in Jesus's name;
for it was He
Who set me free,
and thus my glory came!

So now I'm blessed,
my sins confessed,
assures my entry there,
through heaven's door,
forevermore,
with all God's love to share.

Knock, Knock— Who's There?

Who on my heartstrings is knocking?
The door is open you see.
Long has my misery been locking
and churning inside of me.

Who, in my heart now is pounding?
And sending it up to soar,
this feeling of joy surrounding
my heart as never before!

Who, from my heart now has captured
my sin, my loneliness, and hate?
And saving my soul to rapture—
cometh the judgment date.

Who, in my life now has saved me
from pits of despair, discord?
Who lifts me so sublimely?
'Tis Jesus Christ my Lord!

To Stay in Line

If you lived a life that's full
and met old Father Time;
and you had to push and pull,
I know you stood in line.

For there are lines for everything…
in living as we do;
some with bureaucratic ring
decides what we go through!

But God is not a bureaucrat,
but also has a line,
one that stays just where it's at;
to reach the great sublime.

I know not where in line I stand,
but know I'm near the top,
God drew a line upon the sand
for everybody's spot.

He drew that line upon each birth,
and gave us all a choice;
that while we live upon this earth…
unto His Son rejoice.

And in this line with courage stand
as Christ and Cross define:
always place your trust in Him
or lose your place in line.

The Track Meet

You need not be an athlete
with muscles and the speed,
to leap the hurdles that you meet...
which rise up to impede.
For life is like a track event
that challenge each and all,
the idea is to circumvent...
the chances we may fall.
 For there are many obstacles
that hinders every day,
and through it all I'm bound to call
on God to lead the way.
For if we keep Him in the front,
the route is clear and pure,
and all the things misfortune brings,
will disappear for sure.
So when the race is finished through,
and you met each firm demand,
is your ribbon one of blue?
Or just an "also ran".

Heaven Is Forever Home

I sing aloft my praises as fire within me rages,
for the one I love and call my own;
mine eyes have searched the skies, and Jesus signifies…
that heaven will forever be my home.

Where from His holy tower, He
rules with awesome power,
from the glitter of a golden throne;
where angels spread their wings and hallelujah rings,
all beckons me to heavens home.

Where every soul of race can depend on God's embrace,
as He brings love and hope to those alone;
and sinners can rejoice in atonement for a choice,
that leads to the door of heavens home.

When we all meet in tomorrow, all pain, ills and sorrow,
will nevermore be known,
and beyond the pearly gates to
view God's great estate,
I'll bask in the glory of my home.

So heaven is forever for everyone's endeavor,
and calls for a rise to set the tone,
for an opportunity to be saved eternally…
in heaven, our everlasting home.

A Daily Reminder

Comes oftentimes
When quietness finds
Me in a pensive mood;
I hear a sound
That's so profound…
It brings me solitude.
The sound I hear
Is sweet and free,
A voice so soft and clear,
Calling, calling, calling me
To bring me closer near.
It is the voice of Christ I hear,
I hear him with my heart;
He takes away my woes and fear,
And gives my life new start.
He fills my cup; he lifts me up;
And talks to me each day;
He's here abrupt to interrupt
The ills that come my way.

An Invitation

Oh Lord divine, please come and find
my heart and mind atoned.
Instilled within my hungry soul
is power of Yours alone.

I've seen the light that often cites
the loneliness and strife;
that led me down the path I found…
through sanctity of life.

Come, dear Lord, and fan the flame
that burns within my breast…
forever in your precious name,
I deem my sins confessed.

So here on out without a doubt,
without fear to abhor,
I firmly tread the righteous route
that leads to heaven's door.

Light at the End of the Tunnel

There is light at the end of the tunnel,
the journey is coming to close;
the route was trying and humble,
beset by challenging woes.
Where anger, deception, and torment,
and fear that sickens the soul,
anxiety building a dormant,
like sunshine fighting the mold.

Where loneliness, doubt, resentment…
all swelter in darkness and fear.
but the light at the end of the tunnel
gives hope that Jesus is near.

He waits where light is most gleaming,
to welcome each tormented soul;
His arms wide open, redeeming,
to cast out darkness and cold.
Those hearts that only know sadness,

and some are broken into;
all search for hope and gladness…
to start their life anew.

For that light at the end of the tunnel
is glowing for you and me,
both ends are like a funnel…
that feeds the hope we see.

So it really doesn't matter
which way our travel goes;
both ends the angels gather
in the light that God bestows.

A Place to Embrace

There is a place so long embraced,
it's name is Calvary,
Where Jesus Christ through sacrifice
gave all to set us free.
We cannot tell the pain He felt,
nor suffering that He bore;
but it is true it was for you…
and me forevermore.

He died that we forgiven be,
and from His tender love;
that carries on to heaven's home,
saved by His precious blood.

He was God's son, the only one
to pay the price of sin;
His holy chore…unlock the door
to heaven's joy within.

Oh how He loved, and love we must…
that Christ died not in vain;
just place in Him our faith and trust,
and do so in His name.

Sometime

I stand upon the edge of time,
The distant drums I hear;
Tolling of the bells in chime
Brings me solace here.

I look on high with anxious eye
To search the sky above,
I see God's presence coming nigh,
I feel his warmth and love.

The magic of this moment brings
A joy I've never known,
For soon I'll see the King of kings…
He comes to take me home.

Pleasant View

Lord, Your love and care is fastened in
my eager heart and soul;
and bound within with grace You send
with blessings to behold!

I sing my song of humble praise
in sacred joy to You;
giving thanks for all the ways
You're present in my view.

I see You as a sun-lit sky,
and twinkling stars at night,
the canyons wide, the mountains high,
the trees and foliage bright.

The birds on wing, the songs they sing,
the oceans and the seas.
the forest greens, the lakes and streams,
the winds, and gentle breeze.

I see your presence in each life…
whom tread upon the earth;
domestic, and the human strife,
and those whom live in mirth.

I hear Your voice as gentle rain
that sprinkles on the sill;
like words upon my windowpane,
my hungry soul to fill.

Your scheme of things in all life brings…
a chance for peace and joy,
because You are the King of kings,
my only hope and choice.

My Best Friend

No vast fortune have I made,
nor any claim to fame;
no honor, parade, or serenade
or credit to my name.

Just a simple passerby
who walks among the throng.
No special friends do I rely
of those I pass along.

Just a face within the crowd
of many wandering sheep;
but with much hope to be endowed
by God…His love I keep.

I may not walk with mortal friend,
but not alone I go;
no other voice do I depend…
except this one I know.

For He's Jesus by me walking
along with every step,
It's Jesus, my friend, we're talking,
It's He whom I accept.

Forgiving

Dear God above, with all Your love
You gave Your Son to me;
a friend in deed, my soul in need,
He died to set me free.
Christ braved the cross and took the loss
to save us all from sins,
we must believe as we conceive
His love that never ends.
With special goals to save our souls;
great wonders to perceive.
So let us all be more like Him
and give what we receive.

Light the Way

Dear Lord, please come to me today
and bear my troubles here,
somewhere en route I've lost my way,
I need a course to steer.
The path I'm on is dimly lit,
I hardly see it clear;
I'm treading on it bit by bit
to ease away my fear.
I know Your light is what I need
to brighten up the route,
for every rock that I impede—
I need to sort it out.
I need You now most urgently
to set my compass straight,
so I can handle all I see—
for time is growing late.

The Flame

Lord, I have this passion burning
down deep within my heart;
stemming from years of yearning
and searching for where Thou art.
I've lost my way a plenty
along life's rocky way,
but I counted my blessings many
as I called on You each day.
And the road seems never ending
as I tread each careful step,
avoiding the pitfalls pending,
of which I'm not adept.
'Cause I had my times to falter,
but I tried to do what's right,
and I strove in life to alter
those wrongs I could not sight.
But this flame that I'm attending—
I'll never want to douse;
because I am depending
on the strength that You arouse.
Then someday way up yonder
when the burning will decease,
I will nevermore need wonder—
for I will have my peace.

My Prayer

Lord, come lift me up and bring me
strength to face all problems here;
for peace of mind with joy sublime—
erases all my fear.
You are my Savior, my Reformer
and Redeemer too;
and with Your everlasting love
my life will start anew.

Dear Lord I pray, to Thee I say:
I'm humble as can be;
come be my guiding light today
and live Your life in me.
You are my faith, my hope and peace,
my life and true salvation.
Your very presence in my heart
instills a firm foundation.

So now, dear Lord, I give my thanks
for everything I own,
and everything You've done for me
and family—save none.
And now, dear Lord, I beg of You
to hear my words today,
for what I ask is in Your name,
in Jesus Christ, I pray. Amen

A Time Line

I know I've lived a life of woe,
called "run-of-the-mill."
To feed a fire of lust desire,
my restless heart to fill,
and in that task I came to ask
If God would love me still.
Because I walked a sinners way,
which trail was long and clear;
made every step I took each day
to bring Dear Jesus near.
For He alone, my sins atone,
and this I so revere.
The path of life just goes so far,
my steps have dwindled few,
but there at last, His hand I'll clasp,
for God is waiting true.

My Plea

Oh Lord, can't I have one small amount
of those blessings that I count?
For I've tried hard, I've stood the test,
I always did what You deemed best.
Now it's time to sum it up,
and see how high I filled my cup;
and now in my humble way,
searching peace come every day,
I pray to Thee with anxious heart,
with all my sins to Thee impart.

The Journey Forward

There's a paradise up yonder
where I'm yearning for in wonder,
where I'll meet my precious maker some sweet day;
for I know He's up there waiting
and has my hopes inflating,
as I find my inner peace along the way.

For in this world I've wandered,
and all it's mysteries pondered,
and many times I've felt the sting of pain;
of a heart that has been riven,
but God has so forgiven,
and I've learned to know His love is not in vain.

So from this world departing
I find it so rewarding,
as I sight my golden mansion way up there;
with the blaring trumps blowing,
where my lonely soul is going,
where I hear the harps of angels everywhere!

Where my journey will complete
on a diamond studded street,
at last I'll reach my precious home;
where Jesus, God reside, I will evermore confide,
and from then I know I'll never be alone.

To Cry Out Loud

Tears can be from misery,
like those in stress and strain;
moments when one cannot see
relief from ill and pain.

Tears we get when we regret
that some things will not change;
but live in hope to strive and cope
with courage to sustain.

And there are tears of heartbreak too…
when one feels all alone;
when friends you knew are far and few,
and never call by phone.

Then there are tears as sadness calls,
when loved ones pass away,
and many tears of sorrow falls
in showers of dismay.

But, there are tears of happiness,
of joy and delight;
tears that soothe the heavy breast,
and make the wrong seem right!

Tears of knowing inner peace
that come from when we pray,
for every tear that comes to bear…
will wash the hurt away.

So, go ahead and cry instead
of holding it all in;
and gender has no bearing here,
and crying is no sin!

A Better Choice

Life is not an "easy stake"
as all of us now know It.
Life demands a choice to make,
'tis better not to "blow it!"
For life can be a "piece of cake"…
it's up to us to show it.
but also full of hearts that break,
so trust in God…we owe it!

PART 3:

MEMORIES

Spring Has Sprung

Spring has sprung, yet the early-morning snow
That swept its silent, silver freeze
Across our frigid land...where hung
Icicles, row for row upon the budding apple trees.

Once upon my youth it seemed
That on the first day of spring...
Off came my socks and shoes and with bare feet,
Roam the countryside in blissful dreams,
That each day of life was sweet,
But I blame time for everything...
That changed the world to incomplete.

The changing times that greet us all,
Grips with pleasure, then appall,
Can challenge like a monster's hand
That sweeps us into no-man's land,
But the will and might to set things right
Can make a weakling stand!

So hot or cold, warm or cool
And even wet or dry,
These are the climates of our lives,
And in them all should try...
To greet each day be change or stay,
With will and Godly aims;
In the Lord we trust...in the hope we must,
These things will never change!

Spell of a Waterfront

I sought waterfront and I got it;
I searched for many a day;
not once did I say: "quit"…
'til I found it at Crab Tree Bay.

I love that place on the water,
where I could go boating or fish,
but five years near Swan Quarter,
my children I came to miss.

So I came back to ole Virginia,
where duty is here now to fill,
but I still love the waterfront splendor,
and I plan to go back…and I will!

I think of the beauty down yonder,
where living is sparkled and sweet,
where crabs are measured in wonder,
especially at Mattamuskeet.
Where I could go netting for minnows
from the banks along side the bay,
or catch on my line with some spinners…
some fish that were needed to weigh;
or, I could just sit there in leisure
and enjoy its seawater air;
where quietness of inner peace pleasure…
came into my heart to bear.

But now I've returned to the busy
street traffic, and crowds at the mall;
outdoors, where all is so dizzy,
oh how I'm fighting it all!

Ah, but there is the sake of my children,
who are so much worth the while;
and to forsake my course I'm willin'
to renew here an old lifestyle;
but I'll do it under submission,
'til all my grandkids are grown,
then I'll renew my love mission…
down at my waterfront home.

But for now I'll hold it behind me…
'til I can return once more…
to the place I lived so sublimely…
down on the Pamlico shore!

The Old Grist Mill

Ah, there it is…upon the hill,
beneath that row of pines;
the last remains of Grandpa's mill,
a relic from early times.

See, below the boulders there,
within that small ravine,
the old turn wheel of yesteryear
lies weathered in the stream.

Now, as I view this quaint old place,
a cloak of calm prevails;
remindin' me of joys embraced
with all the pleasant tales.

My memory eye drifts there inside,
back when the grind wheel turned;
where cornmeal from the hull was pried
when on the grind stone churned.

And I recall from long ago
when I was only ten;
Grandpa hitchin' up to tow
with mule and wagon bin.

There across the doorway sill…
in and out he'd dart;
totin' sacks of ground cornmeal
and stackin' on the cart.

And when he got the cart all full,
he'd climb up there on top;
and yank the reigns on that old mule
to go to his first stop.

Perhaps to some quaint market shop
or to a baker's store;
to sell the meal by my grandpop…
to feed the rich and poor.

So there he goes beyond the hill,
my inner eye can view;
pleasant thoughts that linger still
of times that I once knew.

To some, here lies a total mess,
to me, a spot supreme;
of what was once the very best,
still makes my heart serene!

Old Railroad Bill

Old Railroad Bill felt good until
he joined the retired men's luncheon club;
where once a week he went to seek…
solace over buffet grub.

Well, his wish was strong when he came along,
to travel down memory lane;
and he pined to talk of the paths they walked
when making up a daily train.
To reminisce of the life they miss,
just wallow in the golden past.
But—lo, behold—the tales they told…
were about those folks who passed.
And they spoke of Joe and his broken toe,
and Jim, whose hip went out.
Of a clerk named Jake, who for heaven's sake,
came down with a case of gout.

Then there was James with his aches and pains;
and Bob had a heart attack;
and Dick got sick from a home picnic,
and death claimed brother Jack.

So you can see why a guy can be
as down as a swatted fly;
when all that's said is about the dead,
and those who're 'bout to die!
Now Railroad Bill has had his fill,
and I don't mean ham or steak;
for he had enough of that dreadful stuff,
that led old Bill to break.

Well, I suppose he's one of those
who'd rather not dwell on ills,
but use the time for what's sublime,
and not on things that kills!
But Bill was strong, and he said "so long,"
for he wished to part the ways…
from the drear of "spin" to a happy end,
and just dream of the good ole days!

An Evening Stroll

Go to the place where we first met;
a bank on the river's shore.
Two silhouettes in a red sunset
as we stood there years before.
Where we fell in love near a crimson bay;
caught up in a world of bliss,
trading vows that we'd wed someday
and sealed with a tender kiss!

I recall you then, so small and thin,
your hair in a golden bun;
our lives to spend, I knew right then,
that you were the only one.
And wed we did, and the years they slid;
and the gold has turned to gray;
but love, it stayed from the vows we made,
and our bond will never sway.
Now we have two sons, a daughter too,
with twelve grandkids to love;
and tho' our lives will soon be through,
we thank dear God above.
And it shows our care when we stroll back there
to the place where we first met;
to relight the flame that our hearts lay claim,
and the promises we kept!

An Awakening

I was restless in my sleep last night,
but waking up this morning,
I realize how nice and bright
a new day is adorning.

There, the dancing shadows on my wall
from tree limbs in their sway,
bring back memories I recall
in times of yesterday.
Those reflections now remind me
of good times gone before,
of all my days that's left to be,
I'll cherish evermore.
Now I confess life's been a test,
with often "bumps to grind,"
but I intend to do my best
with every way I find.
For in the past sometimes was cast
a dose of life's hard shame,
but just like water in a glass,
'tis water o'er the main.
So, I must greet each coming day
with my best look on life,
by thinking in a faithful way
and not about the strife!

And now, each morning I awake,
come either rain or shine,
I plan to rise and place my stake
in all that's good and fine
To meet the goals that I will set
to carry on my way,
to stay the course without regret,
and look to each new day!

With Every Passing Train

They come from years of toiling
in nights of cold and rain;
through days when heat was boiling;
in times with aches and pain;
from the restless winds of winter
when the countless snow storms blow…
to those gorgeous days that entered…
yield memories that I stow.

But many tales are spinning,
I'll only cite a few;
too many things beginning,
and ending…to review.
When, in '55 it started,
I found the C&O,
and 'til the time I parted
my life was changed I know.
For I loved those years of treading
up the paths beside the track,
coupling air hoses, getting,
and relaying those signals back.
In balmy days of weather,
or snow drifts white and deep,
we made up trains together
for schedules they must keep.

Ah, the sound of engines roaring,
of rambling, rolling steel,
seeing clouds of coal dust soaring…
as we drove cars to the hill!

Where, on the ladders climbing,
and with the grab-irons, hold,
brings back the thoughts reminding
of days gone by of old.
Yet, I hear those hands brakes winding,
and air brakes that were spilled;
that once great massive grinding,
is now so deathly stilled.

Now this railroad yard has feathered
to crews of only three,
where thirty crews once gathered,
now lost eternally!
How could that work explosion
with much tremendous worth,
decline with mass erosion
so quickly from this earth?
This question I'm proposing,
It's "progress" experts claim,
but by bits our railroads' closing
with every passing train.

But in my heart forever
when I look upon the past,
I know my once endeavor
will in my bosom last.
This rumbling tune I'm hearing,
a song with its refrain,
sweet music so endearing
with every passing train!

The Outdoor Privy

If your age is sixty-nine
you may recall the time,
when a little house out back
fulfilled a need.
And in the rain or not,
in weather cold or hot,
you made that blissful journey
through the weed.
There was no shiny chrome,
no marble-laden throne,
just a hole in a bench
to do the deed.

No mirrors on the wall,
just spiders on the crawl,
only dampness and the drear
there to heed.
No TV there in sight,
and only in daylight
was a Sears catalog
you could read.
No water, hot or cold,
no tissues on a roll,
just a catalog or corn cobs,
for the need.
Oh, that little shack out back,
its memory now intact,
has faded from the scene
and gone indeed!

Hands of Time

I keep upon my mantel shelf an old grandfather's clock;
reminds me daily of its wealth
with every tick and tock.
Given to me by my dear dad
the day before he died;
most priceless thing I ever had,
in which I take most pride.
My daddy loved that antique clock
he found in early life;
by trading off a wooden crock
and one dull carving knife.
And proud he was about that deal
he often spoke with pride;
how he made a bargain steal
with smile he could not hide.
And from my youth come thoughts of when
each night at our bed time…
Dad would wind the hands at ten,
and bell that rang the chime.
And now I've come to understand
the symbol in his mind;
for Dad, like any other man
was keeping track—his time.
This same old clock that passed his time
is passing mine away;
this same old tick, tock, and chime
will come my children's way.
And if he or she will come to see
the meaning of its worth;
their measurement of time will be
their joy while here on earth.
For more than just a clock I see;
it shows me every day,
my most treasured memory—
of Dad, who's long away!

Today's Treasures, Tomorrow's Trash

Should your day become depressing
and you want to change your view,
then go into your attic and search
it through and through,
and you will find your worries…shrinking down to few,
by finding something's up there
that once were part of you.
When I entered into mine
to clean things up for spring,
I came upon some boxes wrapped in rotting string.
I brushed away the cobwebs that to those cartons clung;
strung across the rafters where other items hung.
My anticipation soared
as I opened up a box;
the first things I discovered
were our children's baby socks.
Next, their baby clothes and a dehydrated rose,
also hair from curly locks.
A pack of pacifiers, some Sears and Roebuck "flyers"
and a book by Dr. Spock, the one on chicken pox!
Other little frilly things like underwear with laces;

a coat or two, a dress of blue, and
two worn-out suitcases.
Some pairs of jeans, some blues and greens,
and some had stain like traces.
A game of "rook," a photo book
of babies smiling faces.
Also baby shoes in bronze
and uniforms they donned.
They now restore my thoughts of all that we were fond.
Both sons and I in Little League,
as coach and players bond.
I found baseball kits, some bats and
mitts, all I thought were gone.
All our children now are grown,
married with their own.
Forgotten were these tokens—
lost in cardboard's tomb.
These souvenirs bring on the tears—
which grips me to the bone.
But as I sigh, my wife and I realize a job well done.
Another box, inside some frocks, and gown of long ago,
recalls my bride in slowly stride, her face in all its glow.
I found her shoes still shiny bright
and Bible just as white,
with orchid dried below its bow,
and photos of the site—
at wedding's champagne flow.
Beneath that stack, my trousers
black, a tie and coat of white.
Other clothes I thought disposed
and shoes that were too tight.
A wallet worn and britches torn
when bending o'er that night.
All this stuff has held up tough—
lost and long from sight.
Other things discovery brings—
makes my day complete;

old picture frames and model trains
and set of drums we beat.
Crafts we made—now dull and
frayed, boxed up head to feet.
My scrapbooks show that long ago,
my baseball days were sweet.
As I look around I'm duty bound
to keep these items stored;
for come the days which
have dismays,
will spare me from the bored.
But in due time someone will climb
and move this worthless store…
to some landfill beneath some hill,
and gone forevermore.

A Lesson in Humility

There is a fact that's pending
of a tale that has no ending,
and it's always when you think you can't be beat…
in daily work or play or in a contest fray,
a lesser one will come with your defeat.
This tale that I'm revealing,
to me is so appealing,
although this act of fate occurred to me;
that once in '48 these facts I now relate,
how I learned a lesson in humility.
In basketball we won,
we were rated number one;
for two years we didn't lose a game.
As a member I would beam
on this mighty high school team,
to never lose again was our main aim.
But for a special treat
to make their day complete,
we went one night to play this country school;
we went there for their awe—
to prove that we weren't raw,
and to let them see that we were great and cool!
We were cool all right,
'cause the temperature that night
was cold as a pawnbroker's heart;
and when we entered in their small and icy gym,
the thermometer was reading down to naught.
Where there we had to hove
by an old "pot belly" stove—
to warm and thaw our fingers to respond,
and the referees came in to bade the game begin
with overcoats and muffs that they had donned.

And when their team came out,
there rose a hearty shout—
from the sixty-seven people in the stands,
and their players looked so small
in their uniforms and all,
and not once did they come and warm their hands.
And when the game began,
with the basketball they ran,
and they looked like they never played adept,
but every time they shot,
and it seemed an awful lot,
and every time it went right through the net.
And now I must admit
that they gave our team a fit,
and never once again I'll take for granted;
that little country team
who blew our self-esteem,
who gained our respect that they demanded.
And now I see it clear
there is a message here,
that no matter how skilled you come to be;
that if you're great or small
or expert in your call,
there's always someone better you will
see.

An Early Eye-Opener

I was just a little tot in 1933
when I was scooping pecans up
beneath a neighbor's tree.
It was indeed a frightful thing,
the worst I ever saw,
for what appeared is what I feared,
were agents of the law.
A cloudy gust of wind and dust
brought them to the scene,
their sirens on with deafening tone,
their lights were on high beam.
I was so scared
I never dared
to move a single limb,
for now I thought

that I'd been caught
in my atrocious sin.
It's a guilty thing
that fear can bring
but also bring respect,
was when I saw the mighty law
on-rushing to inspect.
And in their flee when reaching me,
kept going right on by…
into the house to aid a spouse
whose husband went awry.
Now from my fright to much delight
I learned a lesson strong.
From deep inside I now describe
there's guilt in doing wrong,
and from the pose from whence I froze
I quickly slipped away,
age six or so I came to know…
that crime will never pay.

Looking Back

I often wonder while in thought
How progress changed our ways,
And all the difference that it brought
From since my childhood days.
Like on Dad's spread of yesteryear
Where yet I see him now,
Trudging along in awkward veer
Behind a mule and plow.
Carefully working down each path
As he plowed back to and fro,
Running into a little wrath
To make that old mule go.
At one end was the shady end
Where Dad would stop the plow,
To take some time to catch his wind
And wipe his sweaty brow.
And he often mumbled at that time…
When resting in the shade,
"Lord, there's got to be another kind
Of tool besides this blade."
Dad never knew the twirling tines
That came to till each row,
And never saw the huge combines
That reap the crops below.
And I suppose in all his dreams
He'd never see the day;
That all those fancy farm machines
Would ever come his way.
No, they were the years of the Model 'T'…
Hard work, the only rule,
The only farm tool Dad would see…
Was the rear end of that mule!

Red's Pier

Near *Huntington Park*, an old landmark,
and just beyond its flank;
lay a strip of land, a beach of sand,
below *James River's* bank.

From out atop that river lot
stood an aging, wooden pier,
which came to be a favorite spot
for people far and near.

There's not a day I pass that way
that memories don't appear;
of thoughts of youth and yesterday...
returns me to *Red's* Pier.

The river, *James*, this pier it claims,
where once our lives were grand,
and across it's lengthy waters came...
a view of the bridge's span;
where sea gulls shrill and anglers thrill
'mid sounds from wind and waves,
all within my heart instill
the joys that memory saves.
Where time to spend a daily trend,
to meet upon *Red's* Pier;
no better place to find a friend
or lose your woes or fear.

There is no clone cleft in stone,
no banner flown in view;
only thoughts of it alone,
marks the place I knew.

A special time now comes to mind,
and with it pleasures bring;
for it was here at Red's Pier
I gave my love her ring.

Since '55 our marriage thrives,
and sometimes shed a tear,
for lasting memory in our lives
of our engagement here;
from where we parked, loudspeakers barked…
Red Crossley's firm demands.
He was heard from dawn to dark…
calling to his hired hands.

Yet, still I hear *Red's* shouts so clear
that come from long ago:
"Donny, Frankie, go out there
and get those boats in tow.
And fill the bin where ice is thin,
and with the box unlock:
and get some bait for those who wait
out on the landing dock.
Take a pail and with it bail,
water from the skiffs about,
and slack the ropes on the larger boats
before the tide goes out."

Through the air these echoes blare
'mid glee from kids at play;
all these things that once I cared,
has long since died away;
but in my heart joy feelings start,
and in my eye, a tear,
for I know I'll never part from
my memories of *Red's* Pier!

My Only Deer Hunt

I never knew the consequence…
slaying a deer would have;
but all the time I felt suspense
while going down that path.

I made a stand up in the trees,
and loaded up my gun;
my hands and feet were 'bout to freeze,
my face already numb.

It had to be the coldest morn
in memory of my years,
 icicles from my nose had formed,
and frozen were my ears.

I was sitting there all tightly drawn
with "big buck" on my mind,
up popped his doe and little fawn,
I thought: "He's close behind!"

That brought surprise at what I saw,
my heart jumped all a-thrill,
my frozen blood began to thaw
on thoughts about a kill!

And there he stood, ten feet away,
whose sad eyes gazed in mine,
I felt a chilling, sick dismay
that traveled up my spine.

I didn't have the heart to fire,
so I just sat and stared,
for I had gained a new desire
to let that deer be spared.

I still don't know the consequence
of having shot a deer,
But, now I feel much better since,
I quit the sport that year.

A Western Dream

I'm driving o'er our western land,
beneath her spacious skies;
around a span of mountains grand
where all the wonder lies.
I did not go by airplane because I wished to see:
all the things that nature brings…in all their beauty be.

Just like a child's first trip to town I'm
struck with rapturous glee;
I come amazed as out I gaze at miracles I see.
Oh, how the mighty mountains rise…
stretched out across the range,
I view the brilliance of their size
beyond the sprawling plains.
Now looking there across the way,
I feel my freedom rise,
and in my heart the joy strings play
of scenes that meet my eyes.

I feel the joy just like a boy, whose egos on the soar,
I realize a paradise I've never seen before.
Driving on, I'm not alone, I feel God's presence nigh;
I ride the brim of rock and rim that peaks along the sky.
and many wonders of the land I
view with humble pride;
Death Valley sand to Canyons Grand,
out to the great divide.

The splendor of the forest greens, the waterfalls in view;
the beauty of the loving things which
makes a dream come true.
My final words, you must take heed
and note this vital tip:
"Do not fly, and with due speed,
take your auto on this trip."

Rocky and Me

I bought this pup and brought him up
and trained him for the trials;
to be the best to win the cup,
 for this, we traveled miles.
My memories of him never dim,
 he was more than just a dog;
all my time was spent with him…
as mist does with the fog.
Day and night we practiced long,
 which was a total grind;
for at first, things all went wrong,
 I thought I'd lose my mind;
'cause Rocky did not understand,
he only wished to play;
even on my reprimand,
he still would want his way.
Now this went on for many a day,
and then, but not complete,
he would respond to what I'd say,
 but not without some treat.

But Rocky came to realize
that treating wasn't all,
my voice of firm, but gentle wise,
was all I need to call.
Our lasting friendship strongly grew
 into one solid bond;
for time came soon that we both knew…
a thing of which we're fond…
of what is just a simple game,
 an exercise at best;
to win the judge's apt acclaim;
to pass his drilling test ;
to be the best dog in the shows
 and take the winner's cup
an acclamation that bestows
upon me and my pup.

I taught him all the moves and tricks
a happy dog it makes;
for this contentment oft restricts
 many of our mistakes.
While training in obedience
this fact remained to be:
that doing this experience,
 same things for him and me;
for wise indeed was Rocky,
 no smarter dog than he,
while I was teaching Rocky,
Rocky was teaching me.
We both were learning self-control,
he, much better than I,
now from the past memories unfold,
lasting until I die.
To place him on any beat:
a sit, a stand or lie;
not even a bitch in cycle heat
 could steal a glancing eye.

He then responds to all commands,
my voice or hand it be;
he'd clear the highest jumping stands
 and then return to me.
I would touch a special thing,
 of leather, metal or wood;
and Rocky knew which one to bring,
 for Rocky understood:
that in a pile of fifteen there,
 placed without inspection,
(for Rocky had not seen)
he just used his scent detection
 with nose so sharply keen.
Then proudly wagging his tail in glee,
when snatching up the one,
the only one touched by me and
 back to me he'd come;
returning item back to me,
 he came in joyful prance,
his eyes as wide as could be,
 his pupils seem to dance.

All this happened long ago and
Rocky is now gone;
but all the thoughts I have in stow,
I'll never be alone.
Rocky left us while in glory
 he was just a young pup then;
on a roadway without gory,
 his precious life would end:
but not before he captured many,
cups and titles that he won,
hearts of love and praise a-plenty,
all agree a job well done.
So from the days of yesteryear
 come thoughts of Rocky's skill.
All our memories now revere…
in our lifetime fill.

Yesteryear's Inflation

The cost to live was almost naught
in days of way back when.
And I will share some of my thoughts
about that time and trend.

It only took a ten cent piece for any show in town,
and while in there, a nickel's fare
bought popcorn by the pound.
And movie flicks were not as sick
as those you see today,
the stars were super, like Gary Cooper,
and beauties like Alice Faye.
A bus to town, a nickel a round,
to visit a ten-cent store,
then a quarter would buy a silk necktie,
well, who could ask for more?

Not any time was spent in line
while in the grocery stores,
and the clerks were good about bagging food,
and they also opened your doors.
Then, there was the butcher's shop we stopped,
no lower prices found.
A pound of chops…twenty cents tops,
and fat back, only five cents a pound.

A Pepsi ad was soft drink's fad,
and it certainly hit the spot,
for just a nickel our thirst buds tickled,
'cause twelve ounces were quite a lot.
And only one cent was all one spent

for just one cigarette.
And brand new cars were cheap as jars,
with 2,000 one could net.

Well, we've come a long way since my heyday,
with cost…now out of sight,
and I must say, without delay,
it will never again be right.

Time Marches On

With every passing moment
lies a chance for us to seize…
a fresh, and new atonement
if we ask on bended knees.
For time is marching on
to meet the judgment date,
and time, it waits for no one,
with the hours growing late.
And for every passing hour,
so precious and so dear,
retains our strength and power
to ban the curse of fear.
So, for every passing minute
let not Satan bar the way,
with heart and soul put in it…
just turn to God and pray.
Now, time is marching on
in a fast and timely rate,
but we won't be alone
when we face the pearly gate.

How Lucky Can You Get?

There's another kind of lotto
where the odds are really great…
in the chances of your being
on your very first birth date.

The odds were so much better
for a billion bucks to win,
but the Lord, and Mom and Dad
chose to let our lives begin.

So, have you stopped to wonder
what a lucky soul you are?
To find yourselves a winner
and still alive…so far.

Well, can't you just imagine
how amazing the event,
that God has given everyone
a life to represent.

But, how so very many lives;
and this I just opine,
they never stop to realize
or give it any time,
to thank the Lord in many ways…
His very precious prize.

So, I suggest we take awhile
and dedicate ourselves…
for everything God's done for us…
before it ever fails.

And don't forget your mom and dad,
their dedicated trust,
for had they chose to separate,
there just would be no us!

In Retrospect

Prologue:
"If your age is under sixty this poem may interest you,
it tells you of the many things in which you never knew.
A timely place in history that is so dear to me,
and if your age is close to mine,
then share this memory"__

A new day is dawning and the year is '34,
a steam locomotive comes rumbling with a roar.
Awakened by its whistle and the odor from the coal,
that swept through my window when I'm six years old.

Our house was on the corner adjacent to the track,
and the fondness of that era is what takes me back…
to the days of radio and *The Lone Ranger* show,
coming to me now as a lone echo:
("Return with me now to those
thrilling days of yesteryear,
from out of the past comes the thundering
hoof-beats of the great horse
Silver, *the Lone Ranger rides again*.")
"High ho, Silver, away we go."
"Get 'em up, Scout," yells his friend, Tonto.)

The two were great in the days back then,
and even got better with *Rin Tin*
a shepherd dog and the best in war
that swept the nation as a movie star.
And *Hop along Cassidy* all dressed in black,
his snow-white hair, and white-haired mare,
this cowboy took no slack.

And only a dime for a show in town
to see *Flash Gordon—to* Mars he's bound.
Buck Rogers came with his space series,
that filled the house on weekend eves.

And see *Ken Maynard* in his huge white hat,
a symbol that the good guys all wore that.
Buck Jones too and *Tim McCoy,*
Lash LaRue, in all their glory.

There are so many more that I could share,
but space allows only some to spare.
So there was those with a different air,
They were the ones with a guitar there.
They sang their way with a pretty song,
yet slung their guns to the black-hat throng.
Roy Rogers and his horse named *Trigge*r,
Gene Autry and his fame got bigger;
both were gentle as a baby lamb,
but tough as nails when it came to stand.

Then those times I'll remember long,
lifestyle images that linger on.
In snow or rain the milkman came,
just as the postmen do,
and the milk and mail and without fail
they always made it through.

And if you chose to ride a bus, a nickel was the fare,
and when in town and look around,
very few cars were there.
The most you saw were *Models "T"* with Chevrolets a few
but soon in time new cars would shine
that changed our world anew.

In summertime and all is hot, the
food stuff needs the cold,
so every home had an nice icebox
that kept the food from mold.
and many times my dad sent me
down to the store for ice,
and if I let the ice block melt, well,
that would not suffice.
Fifteen cents was all it took to buy a smaller block
wrapped in toe bags all the while to stuff in our icebox.

Speaking of ice, it yields a fact,
that the tales I've told to you,
is just a tip of an iceberg here…that years ago was true.
and it's all long gone but the memories strong,
and that's what makes it nice;
because it's now I realize how so lucky I can be,
to live in different times of life,
makes a wise man out of me.

In Hog Heaven

Back in 1947
on the Fourth of July,
I was basking in "hog heaven"
on my first fishing try.
I had never took up fishing,
too busy playing ball,
but my conscience kept insisting
that I answer to the call.

So my brother Mac and I,
with excitement running high,
took off in a rental from Red's Pier;
it was a dinky little boat,
that we made sure it would float,
and a pair of oars to paddle and to steer.
The only things we took
was a string tied to a hook,
some worms and sinkers for the weight;
it was all we need to drop…
to catch some three-pound spot,
or a four-pound croaker on the bait.

We brought up quite a haul…
that enhanced my fishing call,
and I was hooked just like that fish upon my line;
so an addict I became for I longed to come again…
for the sport I discovered so sublime.

Well, more time came on the James,
instead of baseball games,
for I couldn't seem to get enough,
not only for the fish to fill my hunger dish,
but the love and the lust to "fill my cup".

How great it was back then,
with the good times that were in,
with many fishing spots to inspire;
but much has changed since then,
with abundance growing thin,
but the years have not changed my desire.

There's still good spots to go…
like a new pier at *Buckroe*,
or a short drive down to *Hilton's pier*,
or take my cooler "fridge"
to the old *James River Bridge*,
along with my other fishing gear.

Well, I may not catch a lot,
or even one small spot
but I can surely count on this:
that I spent the day away
from the daily grind display,
to wallow in "hog" heaven's total bliss.

A Daily Run

I've tread upon old Newport News
for nigh on sixty years,
I paid my dues, I sang the blues,
I saw both smiles and tears.
And as my thoughts go back in time…
to recall those early days,
the shipyard and the railway line…
by far the two mainstays.
And only two main roads of wrath,
named *Warwick*, *Jefferson*,
on both, I carved a heavy path
that marked my daily run.

I went up one, and came back two,
on every working day.
O'er thirty years I made it through…
to C&O Railway.
To reach this yard and great shipyards,
which Newport News relied;
there came two added boulevards,
named *Mercury* and *J. Clyde*.
But up in time the traffic grind…
has caused so much regret,
now in two-thousand-nine,
great changes have we met.

Like many lanes of torture's pains,
was once a gentle ride;
but progress in its massive gains
have come and multiplied.

But reminisce brings on the bliss;
when thinking of the past,
of good old days I've come to miss,
which still are fading fast!

So when I drive up *Jefferson,*
or *Warwick* by the school,
I recall my "daily run"
without stop lights to duel.

Family Ties

It's hard to put in words somehow
the way I really feel;
to all you dear ones whom I love,
my lips have often sealed.

My heart has always been there,
just kept it out of sight;
with ease I said the wrong thing,
so tough to say it right.

But now I've come to realize,
and open up the door;
to say the things I need to say
that you are looking for.

My thoughts are always of you;
I want things to be right,
I wish to love and shield you
from trouble's gruesome might.

It wasn't that I'm difficult,
nor was I even shy;
but why I acted as I did,
I really don't know why.

I guess I want like everyone,
for harmony to flow;
and never meant no harm to come
nor any ill to show.

But here on out without a doubt
I promise better ways;
to be the person you deserve,
my everlasting days.

So here's a toast to all of you
for putting up with me;
you stayed the course
and saw it through,
and that's my family.

Now I thank you for the good times
you entered in my life;
my love is strong for all you kids,
and mom, my darling wife.

Old Friends

Sometime I pine in loneliness
and wonder where they are,
the ones that filled my memory chest,
my old friends from afar.

I really miss my early years
and folks I knew so well,
and since the time I've seen my peers,
a lot of raindrops fell.

I guess they've gone their separate ways,
as I have traveled mine,
it can't be said just where they stay
this present day and time.

I suppose in retrospect
some joined the great beyond,
while other friends whom I suspect…
still live on Golden Pond.

But I recall from early youth
fond memories do I see,
and I wonder of the truth,
if friends have thought of me.
All together we're just as old
as any souls can be.

'Twas school each day, and work or play,
with many hours spent,
while now I'm gray and so are they,
I wonder where they went.

Have You Seen the Light?

In Virginia there's a little town
and West Point is her name;
where passes through a daily round,
the freight that's hauled by train.
And it was here one rainy night,
the town was sleeping well,
a brakeman with a signal light
just tripped, slipped and fell.
But that was many years ago,
what happened at that time…
when the crewman found himself below
the wheels of 99!

Now every night at West Point site,
a search goes on is said,
this brakeman's plight with signal light,
to find his missing head.

And people come from miles around
to view this strange affair;
they come to town with silence bound
to see the lantern's glare.
Which seems to show the weirdest glow
when flicking in and out;
swinging round and to and fro,
constantly all about.
A ghostly tale upon this rail
that chills the strongest spines.
Of those who come, all will fail
to know why this light shines.

The night must be as black as tar
to view the best in sight,
for just a wink from one bright star,
could dim this mystery light.
A darker night when you can't sight
your hands before your eyes,
is better chance that time is right
for lamplight on the ties.
Now many experts near and far
have tried to solve it out,
by blocking every light and car
for many miles about:
yet, still it shines along the lines
about the railway bed,
looking, searching, for some signs
of his severed, missing, head.
And if you're there you stand and stare,
this thing comes closer yet;
halos in a frost like glare…
just dance in silhouette.
And as the light draws near…you can hear:

footsteps as they squeak;
your heartstrings sear as you freeze in fear,
and you can hardly speak.

Then quietly there as you gaze with dare,
at the light that brightly glows;
It disappears right in thin air…
and where it goes…nobody knows!

Crab Tree Bay

My wife and I once had a dream
which we fulfilled one day;
it came to be our place supreme,
a home on *Crab Tree Bay.*
It is a spot to long behold
with all its beauty here,
where squirrels roam and deer patrol
and also seen are bear.

With many birds and geese abound,
the active otters play;
with Pungo River all around
we fish our lives away;
and when I look across the way,
especially to the west
the sunsets here at *Crab Tree Bay*
are surely at their best.
The colors shown are most divine,
the purple, red, and gray;
nothing meets the eye more fine
as those on *Crab Tree Bay.*
On moonlit nights the water gleams
with sparkles so serene,
in *Crab Tree Bay*, where by all means,
is heaven on earth it seems.
We worked our spot and cleared the lot,
and planted shrubs and trees;
we spent most time in fixing up,
and raking all the leaves.

But, as all things come to end,
six years our length of stay;
our time here is almost up,
reluctantly we say.
A plan has come to interrupt
our lives at *Crab Tree Bay*.
We must me moving on because
destiny calls us back.
We go with slow and painful pause
to lay another tract.

Our love, our thoughts will always beam,
forever will they stay;
within our hearts and every dream
of life at *Crab Tree Bay!*

What Are the Odds?

Now, many people play the odds
in poker, dice, and races;
but there are odds we find in jobs
as well as other cases.

There was a time that comes to mind,
a rare, unusual case;
at work one day on our railway
where fate began its pace.

Sam and I had worked a job
each day the month of June;
and what would later be so odd…
would happen very soon!
Now, speak of odds, you won't believe
this story here I tell;
for Sam and I had planned a leave
from Newport News a spell;
but neither one had spoke of it,
and neither knew each plan…
the entire month while on that shift,
of me and my pal Sam.

So when we left the job that night,
we both went separate ways;
I went home to plan my flight,
and Sam to plan his days.
My destination…Florida,
Clearwater and its beach;
that joins the West Coast corridor,
a thousand miles to reach!

My sidekick Sam had no idea
of my vacation time,
and thoughts of his did not appear,
and never crossed my mind.

So I reached my destination;
Clearwater, then…Tampa Bay,
was there a week's duration,
'til I went to watch a fray;
a baseball game in old St. Pete
some fifty miles away;
the Yankees and the Red Sox meet
in Gratefruit League they play.;
And when the game had ended there
among twelve thousand fans,
two faces met…I do declare!
'Twas mine and my friend Sam's!

My Little Dog Sniffer

He came one day in dreadful cold
with snowdrifts all around;
the winter storm had taken toll
on this small beagle hound.

Upon my back-way stoop he lay,
no whimper could I hear,
for this young pup who went astray,
the end was clearly near.

I gently held…and took him in
to see what I could do.
He looked so weak and deathly thin,
I thought that he was through.

His tiny sides, there was no doubt…
were starved from lack of food;
those bony ribs, they just poked out,
he did not seem to move.

His little body limp as silk…
I placed upon a cot,
and with a bowl of warm whole milk
I nursed him every drop.

And then I saw his little tail
go twitching all around,
then came the best part of this tale,
a new home he had found.

And then on out without a doubt…
this pup began to sprint;
and grow and sprout 'til he was stout,
then to the woods we went.

I've never seen a nose so keen,
he'd sniff out every log.
He was a rabbit chasing thing…
he was a sniffing dog.

Now to the past I look with pride,
no bond was ever swifter…
my once-great prize, that almost died…
my beagle I named Sniffer.

Mom and Dad

Oh, how I miss my mom and dad,
they're in a better land;
they lived for God with all they had,
and now they hold His hand.

They had ways, as we all do,
and now I understand;
their task to raise a stubborn crew,
eight kids to reprimand.

I really wish that they were back
so they could hear me say;
the loving words I kept intact
before they went away.

It wasn't that I didn't care,
respect I did apply;
my words of love were hard to spare
'cause I was mighty shy.

I never could express that word…
called love—we all lay claim,
no better parents did I deserve,
no better friendships came.

When other parents scream and scold,
they'll suffer more than kids,
and good results will not unfold
of what their sanction bids.

But Mom and Dad were both in tune,
and had the best of styles;
instead of fuss and growl and fume,
they spanked us kids with smiles.

They did just what they had in mind;
their chore was not in vain;
the hurt was planned for our behind,
not them to bear the pain.

When they spoke firm with
grinning smile,
it came quite clear to me;
"to spare the rod and spoil the child,"
was not their "cup of tea."

Those times are gone and thoughts I store
adds much to my regret;
that I didn't say "I love you" more
before their time was met.

But when I pray I tell them,
as I say it to the Lord,
for I know that they have joined Him
and all will hear my word.

And now I say to you please heed;
"don't throw your chance away,
but tell your mom and dad indeed:
you love them every day."

PART 4:

IDEALS

Just Let It Go

Confession is resolving
to some degraded soul;
It's lifting when we all confess—
the wayward thoughts we hold.
It helps to build the bridges
instead of stubborn walls;
it buffs away the ridges
in the paths where strife befalls.
To harbor hate, resentment,
held tight within the breast;
will never bring contentment—
'til you get it off your chest!
Then, no matter who may listen;
be Jesus Christ or friend,
confession is the piston
that pumps away the sin.

Two Sense Worth

As everybody knows
there's a reason for the nose;
created for the sense of smell.
And the sense of sight applies
when pertaining to the eyes,
and to the ears for hearing just as well.
Then the tongue was duly placed
to test the strength of taste,
and a set of nerves to touch and feel.
These are the senses five,
God gave us to survive,
but left out two for us to deal!
And they are…learn at our expense
how to use some common sense,
to make it number six upon the list.
Number seven, but not least,
is one that should not cease,
and that's a sense of humor to exist!

If Only One Blessing

Count your blessings all the time
instead of counting years;
this will keep you young of mind
and cut down on your fears.

It does no good to dwell on age,
you're stuck with it for life;
It takes a lifetime to engage,
so live it without strife.

You're only young as you will feel,
or old as you may be;
'tis better to deploy will…
than delve in misery.

We only have one life to live,
and just this one to die;
but we should live as Jesus did,
and surely we must try!

There are many things to do
to smooth the trail along;
one can write a book or two,
or write a pretty song.

We do not have to be afraid
to face our lives ahead,
the better thought here to be weighed:
"Is- better alive than dead!"

We really do not have a choice,
just live the best we can;
and do so with a happy voice
leads to the promised land!

Rungs of Life

Rise ye up, my fallen friend
and brush away the dust;
the fall you had was not that bad,
so try again, you must!
You're young, my friend,
now heed the call…
more rocky steps ahead;
"The bigger they are, the harder they fall"
are only words instead.

And many falls may hurt inside;
so never let them stay;
the pain you feel is in your pride,
just stand up to the fray.

Proverbial "rungs" can lead you up,
or they may bring you down,
but, your "boot straps" are strong enough
to keep you off the ground!

Rungs of life may often yield…
each step a truly test;
so tow the line with all your will,
brings out in you…the best!

Diet My Way

So, you want to do a diet
and you don't know how to start?
Well, here's my way to try it
and I hope you will take part.
First, on every morn
when you open up your eyes,
you look upon your mirror form
the minute that you rise.
Now gaze upon your body and evaluate your size,
if the sight reveals you're shoddy,
or in some great demise,
then instead of drinking toddy,
do a morning exercise!
And do these calisthenics, friend
with outlook that is wise,
you do them in your house but spend
some time beneath the skies.
Where you do a lot of walking there
each day with longer strides.
If action is your highest gear,
you'll lose it in the thighs!
But, now please take another look,
I think you will surmise,
that your habits in the dining nook
should come as no surprise;
for you need to cut your eating down
In order to survive,
and that means smaller portions found
In all your food supplies.
So now at breakfast time
you choose the smallest size,
'cause the morning meals define

a portion that decries—
of one small bowl of bran buds—
that hardly satisfies;
but you need those fiber grubs
for your system to revise.
And now it's time for dinner
where you have the largest eyes,
but fish will make you slimmer—
than those sausage pizza pies.
But you have to stay in training,
and do what's best and wise;
so you eat your fish retaining
the secret to down size.
Now supper is the time that brings
the rich and greatest prize,
a great big bowl of salad greens
where all the nutrients lies.
The salads take away the lows
and bring about the highs;
by now you are reducing clothes
and saying last good-byes—
to all the weight that you disposed
on all you gals and guys!

String Along

Anything is possible,
but nothing is for sure.
Life is full of strings to pull
to make your troubles fewer.
The secret is to separate
the different strings you hold;
investigate, then activate
the ones that fit your mould.

The String of Woe is #1…
Let's color it with red,
but leave it on its spool undone,
avoiding things you dread.

The String of Hope is #2,
a strength of solid test;
paint this one a pretty blue,
and tie it to your vest.

The best of all is #3,
for Love is what it means,
wear this one where all can see
its color shade of green.

View these so-called strings of life,
the ones you pull with friends,
just toss 'em all that brings you strife,
and pull the string that wins!

Sugar and Spice

From the pantry of our lives comes
the sugar and the spice.
the recipe below should well suffice.
Ingredients galore for both the rich and poor,
so be careful how you handle yours.

For sometimes there's sugar,
and sometimes there's salt;
adding something bitter
spins a web in which we're caught!
But in their definition
each one can be too much;
like flies who meet disaster
within a spider's clutch!

Too much sweetness can project
a sense of false pretense,
something like a mask effect
to shield one's lack of sense.
Too much salt can decimate
and melt the coldest ice;
and make the blood evaporate
as well as friends alike!

Too much bitter will produce:
"a bad taste in one's mouth,"
a known cliché, old and true,
but literally no doubt!
So use them all, but one by one…
just keep them low in count;
will brush away life's web we spun
with just the right amount!

Friendly Quiz

On a scale from 1 to 10…
choose a number from within,
that represents a true friend in your life;
not including those…
like your neighbors who impose,
or people whom just smile and waves.
I'm referring to the one
who always seem to come
when problems cause dismay on trying days.

It's just a simple check
to determine the respect…
that's given when you're down and out;
considering of course
that you always show remorse…
as a friend to other folks in doubt.

When a friend shows up indeed
for another friend in need,
nothing can be better for the soul;
but if no one else is there
in times of cold despair,
welcome to the millions in the fold!

And I suppose it's so…
that the count is very low,
for a true friend is difficult to find;
but even if it's one,
'tis a better count than none,
when self-esteem is riding on the line!

And if your count is naught,
and in turmoil you are caught,
I suggest there's one you can depend,
for He's really #1,
God's gift and only son,
Jesus Christ, forever our true friend!

Ladder to Success

You cannot get ahead
'less you use the one you got;
for the journey that you tread
is a long way to the top.

With every step you climb
will come moments of despair,
just keep your goals in mind…
pray the Lord will get you there.

And when you reach the top,
there is nowhere else to go,
but back to your starting spot
that beckons you below.

For there awaits the tatter
as you face your daily chore,
to lead you down the ladder
that you had climbed before.

So now you need a buffer
as the challenges appear,
for life can be much tougher
if success is met with fear.

So build a buffer zone
to keep your calling sound,
to hold your very own
when ill winds blow around.

For if you lose your touch,
and your world comes tumbling down;
it's not the fall that hurts so much
as that of hitting ground.

"Best be safe than sorrow,"
when you find some loosen rungs,
don't wait until tomorrow,
for tomorrow never comes.

Just fix the problem mess
before they take a hold;
makes the ladder of success
your everlasting goal!

Music in the Rain

Like tinkling tones from vibraphones
come sprinkles of the rain;
softly, gently pinging tunes
upon my windowpane.
Then silence of my room succumbs
unto a blissful air;
a simple mood of solitude
that lends itself to care.

How little things can mean a lot
in lieu of so much stress,
the magnitude of one raindrop
can soothe a burdened breast.
And then upon my Quonset hut,
in downpour sheets they came,
roaring like a drummer's touch
upon the metal frame.

And can't you just imagine,
a multitude of bells
chiming in a group on a hot tin roof,
thrilling as the music swells?

Brings me solace to my ear,
and comfort to my brain;
to lie in rapture that I hear…
a melody's refrain, a chill I can't explain…
seems all my troubles disappear.

Then off to "slumber land" for dreams,
all free from ill and pain,
oblivious to the world of things,
except the falling rain!

Just Breeze to It

Not a single Christmas toy
that I got when just a boy,
can match the inner joy I now embrace;
for the sprinkles on my brow
reflecting o'er the bow,
raises my goose-pimples as it sprays.
As I cruise out toward the bay,
I honestly can say:
"I can't find a way that explains…
sensations that I feel
when I get behind the wheel
to steer my 19-footer through the James.
In my sturdy old "Proline"
as I glide across the brine,
nothing else on earth seems to care;
except the beauty of the scene,
with the sky and sea serene,
and the breeze that trickles through the air!
And there is much to gain
if you set your plan and aim,
toss away your troubles and just Go!
And out here you will find
a welcomed peace of mind,
just wallow in contentment with the flow.

So when you start your motion
out to the deep-blue ocean,
always keep this thought in mind:
"you can fish if you wish,
only ride if you decide"
either way your life becomes sublime!

Roses or Thorns?

To every living person a moment will arrive;
to do what's good or evil,
with a cross, or cross denied!
The strain of life's behavior
offers up a rose or thorn;
and the choice is never ending…
where light and dark are borne.

And the light is ever glowing
that reveals the blood of Christ,
which is adding up new crosses
to seek eternal life.
New choices and new chances…
when time will only tell,
and the good should never falter…
for hope and faith to dwell.

Yet, the evil still may prosper,
with truth they often scorn;
Truth, forever on the rose,
false, forever on the thorn.
Thorns, the crown they placed upon Him,
to mock the truth and light,
to shame the roses blooming
to kill with evil's blight.

Yet, the rose may fade and wither,
but within that darken time,
'tis God above us standing,
'til again the roses climb!

Why?

Why is "why" a question?
Well, I think I know why!
We all have no conception
upon which to rely.
Some ask why of many things
that none can understand,
yet, when they get an answering,
they ask: "Why are you so bland?"
But why is not important,
it's the answer that will count;
and if you have no answer,
just silence your account.

Below are questions often posed,
I'll just cite a few;
"Why is the sky so often blue
with such a brilliant hue?
especially when it's all sunlight
and no clouds are in view."

"Why does the ocean roar
and why it changes tide?
And why you hear it from a shell,
the roar from deep inside."

And "Why is the earth so round
when seen so flat and wide?
and why does it spin around
while no one feels the ride?"

"Why are all the snowflakes
a mystery to the mind?
while having six dimensions,
none have the same design."

One can ask why to anything,
even ask why to why;
no simple answers does it bring,
most folks don't even try!
Why is there anything?
The answer lies above;
The hands of God, our only king,
and by His trust and love.

So why is "why" the question
in the heart of unknown things?
God provides the mercy
that He forever brings.
The trust which we rely,
is the essence to comply…
without the use of why!

The Homecoming

There were tears mid jubilation
as the soldiers came to dock,
a welcomed celebration
for those who fought Iraq.
Both women and the men,
and the wide smiles they wore,
arriving home again
to the loved ones they adore.

Came an air of praise and honor
for the duties they performed;
not like the times Jane Fonda
led the activist in scorn.
But now 'twas hugs and kisses
with huge joy on display;
the public bade good wishes,
with goodwill here to stay.

So welcome home a mighty force
who fought a war with pride;
fighting on a deadly course
so freedom could survive.
But there are some returning

with wounds that creep for life,
but show a heart still yearning
to get back in the fight!

And there was one marine
who was searching for his wife,

he was calling out her name,
for he had lost his sight.
And when they finally met
came an embrace so profound;
their cheeks were soaking wet
from the teardrops falling down.

I heard the words he said
to his lovely wife, Marie:
"It's better to be blind than dead,
and I'm happy as can be."
And then they disappeared…
arm and arm among the throng,
while others on the pier
look for families they belong.

Now don't forget the fallen,
may there memory never wan;
they met their duty calling
and did not die in vain!
And now they rest in heaven
by the welcome hand of Christ,
a celebration given
for their eternal life.

This jubilee has come and gone
and again we must band;
another war is going strong
inside Afghanistan;
which we must wait to celebrate;
but proudly we will stand,
support our troops to build their faith…
'til they come home again!

Just Plain Words

Now you do not need a "hanky"
when you read my poem here;
it's nonsense but so true,
and I thought it nice to share.
For long I've held an interest
in the way a thing occurs;
like the odds that something happens
and the mystery it refers.

And the reason that I notice
is it happens all the time;
the event is so amazing,
it would boggle any mind.

There are others I could mention,
but this one takes the cake;
it's logic so uncanny…
no sense here does it make.
Now the odds in this event…
should it happen only once;
would be a trillion number
to the viewer it confronts.

Now maybe you have seen it
if you do what I do,
I'm reading or I'm writing,
and TV is on too!
And this is when it happens
as a word comes to my mind,
and a voice from the TV says…
the same word at that time.

Sometimes it happens once,
and often two or three,
and I begin to wonder
if fate is tricking me!
Now stop and just imagine
of how many words there are;
all vocabularies present
would string a line to Mars!
That someone in a TV show,
and many miles away;
speaking several thousand words…
would timely come to say…
any word I'm reading or any one I write;
pops up bright and jolting
like a bolting lightning strike!

Since the odds are so terrific,
with no way to comprehend;
I'll just add it to all mysteries
that life has to contend!

The Highest Peak

There is an adage old,
one you may recall:
that "Into every life
some rain must fall,",
but here's another message
that one can always find:
that "There are higher mountains
that everyone must climb."

Many torturous mountains
of turmoil and stress,
appearing in lives to challenge
and to test!
Every living person at some point in time,
will face a high-peaked mountain
that boggles the mind.
Where each may know rejection,
loneliness and doubt,
with struggles and life's puzzles
to figure it all out!
But solid faith of travel
o'er those weary roads to trod,
will bond a strength of courage
with almighty God.
Within His schemes of planning
lies wonderful things…
which He provides us with…
many choices supreme;
not fretting now or quitting,
but strive on to climb…
to reach the highest summit
and rejoice there divine!

But the trails will be rocky
with pitfalls abound;
but Jesus will be guiding
on our way to a crown…
with the one whom we love
who is waiting there on high
at the peak of our mountain
in the sweet bye and bye!

The Good Old USA

Yes, I love the U S A
with rapture in my faith.
I dedicate both heart and soul
to each beloved state;
to everyone, the young and old,
where pride is ever great.

I pledge allegiance in her name,
the U S true and free;
'tis here where brave men staked their claim
to start our history;
those pioneers whom early came
will live eternally.

So sing my praise to U S A;
where spirits ever bloom…
as does the flowering forest trees
where song birds croon their tunes,
and from the purple mountain's breeze,
drifts blossom's sweet perfumes.

The U S A for evermore
be glorious and grand,
where folks of races live as one
in our most treasured land;
to find a place here in the sun,
with peace to every man!

An Inner Voice

There's a deeper voice inside
that lends itself to guide,
but often leaves us all confused,
for in our oft endeavors
when we doubt our shoulds or whethers,
someone usually gets abused!

So it's up to each deciding
that a problem may be chiding…
when it shows it has that sort of ring;
so deny that inner voice
when in doubt about a choice;
just give a smile and don't say anything!

For that little voice inside
may not be cut and dried
stemming from your mind's inner eye,
So in understanding this,
you will never be amiss,
and never need this voice to rely!

The Sound of Music

I guess I'm still old-fashioned
when it comes to modern trends;
especially of the noise
and the message that it sends.
Within the sound of music
lies a racket worst of all.
The drums go loudly banging,
with cymbals clashing, clanging,
and some weirdo at the mike
screams and squalls!
And as the guitar players strum
and the sound is like a bomb,
the lights go up and the air
is filled with smoke,
with singers yelling here
and belly dancers there;
that's the sound of music, folks!

Noise, noise, noise,
the trend that so annoys,
one hears it in the lyrics and the themes,
when a voice screams and cracks,
which makes my nerves react,
it's time to shut it off by all means!
Here's the tip I give to you,
it's the one that I do:
when commercials on TV bang and yell;
is quickly mute the thing,
which suddenly will bring…
the precious sound of silence ever felt!

Now, there's things we have no choice,
when it comes to deal with noise
like traffic on the rise,
and echoes fill the skies,
with autos and rescues every day;
but the ones that gets me more
are the blowers from outdoors,
by neighbors blowing leaves away!
They send a certain sound
that penetrates around,
to every eardrum, far and near,
except the folks who use,
their hearing is defused,
all I can do is plug my ears.

Oh where, and oh where
have those splendid voices gone?
the ones that soothed the soul,
like that of *Nat King Cole*,
who put the magic tone in every song.
And the music calmed the day
when *Sinatra* sang "My Way"
and what's a Christmas time without *"Bing."*
And the most adoring choice
is *Perry Como's* voice,
oh, how that man could sing!
But what we have here now
is a noise making crowd;
where the racket of it all amplifies;
they need not sing a word
since none of them are heard,
which adds to the misery it supplies.

Well, maybe one more time
comes the sound of music fine,
when melodies and lyrics offer peace,
so until that time and span
I'll keep the "mute" in hand,
and find some fifties oldies on release!

To Bobbie, My Wife

What can I do my dear to prove my love for you?
What would it take for me to make
your dreams of joy come true?
If I could gather every star,
the moon with all its hue,
the silver-coated clouds afar,
I'd give them all to you;
and also add the entire world
'twould be a small amount,
for all the splendor you unfurl
is just too much to count!

You stayed by me in thick and thin,
you're always at my side,
my love for you will never end
just like the ocean tide.
As sure as stars come out at night
and sunlight brings the day;
I'll hold you to my bosom tight,
and in my heart to stay.

So, my dear wife, I humbly say:
I owe my life to you.
for all support that you display
each day our whole life through.
You gave me strength when I was weak,
you answered every call;
was there when times were dark and bleak
to catch me should I fall,

You're more than just a wife to me,
my friend and helper too,
you're there to look when I can't see…
in many things I do.

So as we live our love will blend
as we continue on;
and while you're with me to the end,
I'll never feel alone;
and even tho' in times of woe,
there may have come some sparks,
but none of them would last you know,
'cause our marriage still embarks.
Years, fifty-two, each day I knew
would bring a brand-new start,
and with a angel just like you…
to love with all my heart!

Spell of a Sunset

The twilight shadows cast their spell
by sunset's golden ray;
and I, in mystic solace dwell
'mid magic of God's way.
How beautiful this awesome sight
that fills my wondrous gaze…
Ah, the beauty of this spectrum light
just takes my breath away!

Across the water's silent span,
the flame reveals its gleam,
a mirror of a grandeur land
in my celestial dream.
As creeping shadows slowly wane,
my troubles disappear,
for it is here in God's domain
I lose all my despair!

Now special shadows cast a spell
when shown by heaven's light,
and some are shadows of ourselves,
which fade into the night!

Rise and Shine

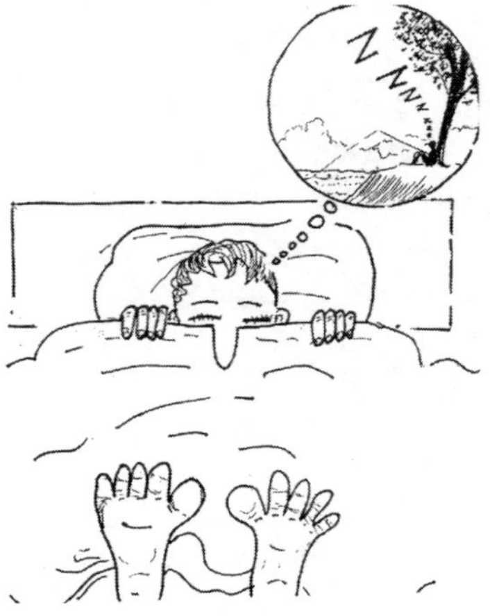

It's so easy to be anxious
when you feel you're down and out,
and the problem is much greater
when the cause is fear and doubt!

But it's not the fall that hurts you,
it's the getting up that counts;
not the misery when you wallow,
but the spring that's in your bounce!

It's not the way you spend your money
nor how much you need to save,
but the honest way you earned it
and the charity you gave.

'Tis not the fear that seems to rob you,
nor the doubt that lies within;
but undying faith God gave you—
so go share it with a friend!

Just a Cover

There's a pit bull on our street…
who snarls, and shows his teeth
every time I pass him in his yard.
He shows it pure and plain
that he's king of his domain,
that I should watch my step and be on guard.

It's the natural thing to do,
but there's something else here too;
his bark is much greater than his bite;
for when I gave to him
the kindness of a friend,
he stopped and wagged his tail just like a kite!

Now, there's a moral to this tale
that's occurring without fail,
consider this to people whom have fault;
of a saying old and new,
for it's absolutely true,
"you can draw more flies with honey than with salt "

So, don't raise any ire
feeding fuel to the fire,
by adding to the ruckus like some do.
Just show some kindness and respect
to the ones that you detect…
as having that impartial attitude.

For, like that cagey old pit bull,
some are trying hard to pull:
"the wool over everybody's eyes,"
and when you don't give in,
but show your love within,
it always brings them down to size!

Catch a Falling Star

'Tis said that in the heavens
of the stars we view from earth,
each represents a person
whom God assigns at birth.
Yes, those countless stars a-gleaming,
there's one for you and me,
every twinkle has a meaning
that figures God's decree.
Which means our souls rejoices
in everlasting life;
by making best of choices;
accepting Jesus Christ!

That when a life is passing,
some see a streaming light,
and someone says: "God's catching…
a falling star tonight!"

The Leaning Post

Dwell ye not in woeful somber,
though the world seems hard and mean,
delve in thoughts of hope…to ponder…
that's a post on which to lean.
Thoughts that change your way of thinking;
things that lifts your self-esteem…
like dear friends whom you are linking,
there's your post on which to lean.
Find a post that be your token;
better yet…ye be the host;
hold the hands of those heartbroken,
you become their leaning post.
There are many posts of lumber,
 they are set in earthly sod,
but far best…to cure our somber,
stands the leaning post of God!

Up an' at 'Em

When you rise in early morn,
are there thoughts of what to do?
like doing chores where bliss is born,
that makes your life feel new.
How 'bout jobs that brings rewards
that keeps your mind at peace,
like mowing grass or seed the yards,
or walking your dog on leash.
Or building a simple blue birdhouse,
or painting your wood shed red.
Get your spirits to really arouse
by painting your house instead.
A thousand things that joy here brings,
that's calling for your hand,
so remove ye from those inner springs,
and rise to do what's grand!
If you perform what I suggest,
then I know you're not a dub,
'cause they're the deeds
we love the best,
so welcome to the club!

The Outdoors Man

I truly love the great outdoors,
a life I've always known;
my heart takes wings like an eagle soars
when I hear old nature's tone.
So give me the good old back hill roads,
the rolling meadowlands;
the back-wood creeks where the fish abodes,
or the beach with its golden sands.
Or spend the day on Chesapeake Bay
and dream of all that's grand;
just wish the world would go away
and return on my command!
Or go to the busy woodlands free
down deep in the forest glade;
just breathe the air of ecstasy
of the life here God has made.

Just hear the breeze in the tall pine trees,
or listen to the whippoorwill,
or smell the dew on the fallen leaves,
or remains of an old wood mill.
So give me the good old outdoor life,
not that of the busy town;
removed away from the ills of strife,
just buried in the joys I've found!

Just a Matter of Time

I'm waiting for my ship
which hasn't yet come in;
but in my heart I know it won't be long,
for even as I pine of this dream boat on my mind,
the echo of its steam horn sings my song!
Now, in my anxious view
as I gaze across the blue,
I see her silhouette against the sky:
where across horizon's zone with a cargo all my own,
she's bringing home to me—my "piece of pie."
There! beyond the foam, I glimpse her coming home—
steaming on to fill these goals of mine.
I'm caught up in a trance and the butterflies all dance
as she speeds along across the brine.
And soon I'll ride her bow and
we'll sail on here and now
and brush away the ocean's spray;
and when she carries me to my port of destiny—
I'll be king of my domain—as winners say!

A New Look

Some never know what they really can do,
unless they gives it a go;
they can wish all they may
and daydream away,
but just wishin' won't make it so.
With talents galore, but hidden in store;
like that in a buried drum;
rests strong and the frail
whom surely will fail,
just wishin' for things to be done.

So, grab some brushes and paint,
and don't say you "cain't,"
for this word is not in the book;
and color the things that come in your dreams,
will show how good you can look.

Next, say what you think
with your pen and the ink,
expressing just how you feel;
then fix in your mind some wording that rhyme,
those that will fit the bill!

Now here's an adage as clear as a bell;
one referring to doubt;
that "if you don't try, you'll only get by,"
which isn't enough to shout;
that…"pitch it on in, and try it again,
if first you don't succeed;
that in the end you'll always win,
if you keep on planting the seed!"

And after it's done you've proven someone,
could do what he thought he couldn't;
and that only to try, and understand why:
"that proof lies there in the puddin'!"

A Summer Song

It's a song I sing in summer,
for the heat is so severe;
a same old line at wintertime
in wishing summer here.
It's the same old tune of many,
I suppose I'm worst of all;
for through the cold it's heat I seek,
when hot, can't wait for fall!

I guess I'm self-divided,
and can't make up my mind;
but God provides and takes all sides,
a choice for all mankind.
It's just too hot to garden,
high temperatures prevail,
like a warden fenced in cordon,
I'm free, but still in jail.

And the weeds have taken over,
'cause it's too darn hot to "weed,"
and the lawn is so, no need to mow,
for the drought has killed the seed.
So I'm forced back in confinement,
back where the room is cold,
back to my chair to sit and stare,
at my TV of old.
And sit in total pleasure,
and dream of snow and ice,
and just pretend and wallow in
the nicety of life.

And dream of snowflakes falling,
the children on their sleighs,
the snowball fights, the Christmas lights,
brings back my childhood days.

But if I sit here long enough,
fall will come anon,
then 'mid the trees and falling leaves
I'll relish all I'm fond.
But—lo, behold—comes winter cold,
and I'm right back to be tied;
in my living room, the same old tune:
It's too darn cold outside.

Winter Song

I know it's in God's scheme of things
so please don't take me wrong,
for every day that comes my way
I cherish all day long.
Even in the wintertime
deep down I feel rejoice;
and dearest God has given nod
so I can make a choice.
To choose between a hot or cold,
it won't take long for that;
for winter squalls; and indoor walls,
confine me where I'm at.

Within my lonely cabin here
I'm "blue" with anxious wait;
and like a bear cooped in a lair,
I'm bound to hibernate.
I dread the long, hard winter months;
unrest has taken toll.
I sit and pine for summertime
to thaw my frozen soul.
The snow outside has risen high
and banked up to the sill;
I'm hunkered in a prison den,
with only time to fill.
I gaze upon the dark-gray skies,
and think of summers old;
then the Ground Hog came, his shadow claims
six more weeks of cold.
Well, I've weathered storms
of wind-blown cold;

and sure as sun will shine;
as sure as night, and stars are bright,
will come the warm springtime.

To embrace all of nature's call,
the fragrance of the grass;
the joys that come when spring has sprung,
with cold days gone at last.
So spring has come and life has sprung,
and beauty fills the skies…
with bumblebees, and budding leaves,
and pretty butterflies.
And purple martins on the soar,
The humming birds in flight;
The mocking bird, whose song is heard,
makes everything seem right.

Just breathe aroma from the vines
from nature's sweet perfumes;
makes my heart sing: "How Great the King,"
Creator of all blooms.

So, now to get my walking shoes,
my thoughts are all out door;
I cannot wait to celebrate
the springtime I adore.
And bask along in huge content
while treading nature's trail,
an inner voice with much rejoice,
is saying: "all is well."

A White Remedy

It's a trend that seems to show…
it's therapy with snow;
bringing forth delight from young and old,
a stimulus of kinds…
that brightens darken minds;
resurrecting life unto the soul.

On a bleak and rainy day,
may bring somber on display,
suggesting people stay in bed;
but the snow!
The white and falling snow,
awakens weary hearts instead.

One can see it everywhere,
you can see it on the air;
and telephones are ringing off the hook;
people calling folks they know…
if they know about the snow,
a great chance to vent…they overtook.

What about the snow
that brings out all the glow?
Maybe it's because it's rarely seen;
or is it just a cause
to give us chance to pause,
oblivious to our woes…and just dream!

A Tribute to Sean

A bundle of joy was he,
as happy a lad can be.
he would light up your world
when antics unfurl,
with sparkle we all agree.

As a child he captured your soul,
with manners too playful to scold,
he scattered around everything he found,
which wrecked our entire household!

His hands you see, as busy a bee
in search of his place in life,
explore and adore…Sean's daily chore,
oblivious to woe and strife.

Which mattered no way, 'twas learning display,
and the cost was only a broom,
We picked up things that each day brings…
and it all would end too soon.

And at age sixteen, a mid-age teen,
a life that's not yet grown,
by the light of dawn, the Lord called Sean,
to heaven and his home.
So the luster of life has met its demise,
his grin and the smiles are gone;
but not in our hearts which never departs
the memories we keep of Sean.

A Blossom Fell

In the trees of life
Sweet flowers dwell;
Within our own
A blossom fell,
Giving way to the will of God…
Forever young within the sod.

Yet, The blossom fell
And set the seed
To grow again some soul in need,
And there upon a lonely hill
A tree will rise which blossoms fill;
Some may wilt and fall away,
But nothing dies, it is God's will.

Life's Contestants

Life is merely a contest
where simple rules apply,
and all contestants entered
will need to qualify;
by living with certain standards
that's judged from heaven's eye.

The rules are really easy
and many to comprehend;
in test of might to do what's right
that no rule shall suspend,
to grade one's will endurance…
and everyone can win!

In this game of life competing
and with it's rules comply;
just please the one who's judging,
He will end it all a tie,
and all the first place honors
will come from God on high.

Leave 'Em Alone

There is a magical splendor
that seems to grip us all;
when cold winds blow and fire lights glow,
when leaves begin to fall.
We find our glee in ecstasy,
but restless is our spell,
for now I gaze into a maze
of golden leaves that fell.
When leaves have died I peer outside
and view them all around;
it's time to go because I know
that more is coming down.

Without ado and spirit new
I feel the calling now;
although the wind may not descend,
I'll rake 'em anyhow.
So out I go to meet the flow
of leaves from everywhere;
and for a while I had a pile,
but now they're up in air.

But never mind, there's more to find,
it's early in their fall;
for months it takes and many rakes
before I get them all.
It's all for room which I assume
allows for many more;
so on I rake for just fun's sake…
that raking has in store.

Yet, still they fall and sail and sprawl
in showers of display;
and on and on the leaves are blown,
but I'm raking anyway.
But this is fall, I meet my call,
but I am not alone;
'cause from my view I see you
out raking leaves that's blown.
Wow, Still they come, it's never done,
this raking, raking on,
and now it's I who wonders why
that I became so prone.

A lot of leaves from other trees,
from other homes around,
are here from winds that blows and sends
them straight to my home ground.

But I am bound to rake the ground,
although it sweats my brow;
to rake in winds, which never ends,
but I'm raking anyhow.

But what if we should wait and see…
just where the leaves end up;
and only then we'll know just when…
to say: "enough's enough"

In Need of Repair

I'm stranded by the lone roadside,
my motor just conked out.
My route had been a rocky ride
of many miles about.

I've been driven, pushed, and tampered with,
and left out in the cold.
I've given all that I can give,
my parts are getting old.

I need a new replacement valve,
my fuel is all burned out;
this trouble that I'm facing now
is leaving me in doubt.

My battery needs recharging
and the strength is mighty weak.
It's given all that I demand,
it's reached a final peak.

If I could get another coil
more sparkle would revolve,
and there would be less tug and toil,
and problems would resolve.

A brand-new starter would begin
to start my life anew;
and bring my strength to go again
with freshness I once knew.

For all these parts I need thus far,
the reason is you see;
they're not really for my car,
but repairs that's meant for me.

One More Jewel

"This is the last, there'll be no more,"
our children so had stated,
but that's a song we heard before,
their tune is now outdated.

A great-grandson comes in the fold;
our egos now inflate;
one more wonder to behold,
again, our hearts elate.

One more jewel for us to tend;
adds sparkles to our crown;
this brings the sum to number ten
to spread sweet joy around.

One more set of tracking feet;
(ten will come with smacking lips)
carpet floors to clean and sweep
from rounds of ice cream dips.

Add one pair of rosy cheeks,
glowing as their joys unfurl,
We, giving what their young hearts seek,
"I wouldn't change this for the world."

All this makes us oh so happy,
all our grand kids to adore,
these special gifts for this Grand "Pappy"
and *Grand Ma* forevermore.

The Robbers

I have a feeder, nice and new,
all set and full of seed;
I'm looking through my window's view
for birds to come and feed.
Here comes the birds, but also herds
of squirrels that show for lunch;
they creep and merge and then a surge
around the post to bunch;
then climb the post, scare off the hosts,
devour the entire seed.

They flip and flop, jump to the top
and swing around the side;
and then they'll stop and then they'll drop
and then they run and hide.

"I'll make amends, fine-feathered friends,
I'll try to intervene;
I'll lend a hand and tie a band
and to that…add a screen."
Then came the squirrels, their tails all curled
in usual sneaky styles;
and feathered friends up on the limbs
are chirping loud and wild.
But soon their swoon turns into gloom
while looking on the scene;
for furry friends had leaped from limbs
and landed on that screen.

So gone indeed is all the seed;
"I'll need to think this through;
to find a lead to stop this breed;
this furry, mischief crew."
So now I set a fishing net
above the feeder coop;
but still they jump up from a stump
back in the seed to root!
And all around, the birds, they frown,
they peck, peep, and pine;
and now I'm bound to find what's sound,
a final stop to find.

So, smart and shrewd I fix a tube
around the feeders prop,
twelve inches round, twelve inches down,
and lid that seals the top.
It's now they find that when they climb
there is nowhere to go;
for they cannot move while in this tube,
no way but back below!
And now the birds, their cheers are heard,
their glee is clearly sent;
'cause squirrels around eat seed aground,
now everyone's content!

Man's Best Friend

They wag their tails and not their tongues
are why these pets are grand;
no better friendships ever sprung
as that of dog and man.
They never show a scornful trait,
and cannot fume and fuss;
They have no way to issue hate,
just love with willing trust.

They're always there to show respect
and faithful to your call,
quickly to your side—protect
if harm should ever fall.
They cannot argue politics,
complain of what they eat;
just responds with friendly licks
when given special treat.

And how mine looks so pitiful
when comes my dinnertime,
He will sit with mouth a-drool
and eyes with wishful shine!
His pupils dance like silhouettes
you see on curtain shades;
restless, eager, that he gets
the morsels that he craves.

So therein lies the bond of two,
both willing to depend;
on either one to keep anew—
the love that lies within!

Analogy Food for Thought

You cannot make a garden grow
without the proper care.
You cannot force a horse to drink,
but you can lead him there.
You cannot run away and hide
when there's no place to go;
that shields a guilty circumstance
that only you may know.
This is the way life really turns
when dealing with a trend;
to find solutions to the cause,
the answers lie within:
each heart and mind of everyone
must meet the task at hand.

First, you tend the garden bed
and purify the land,
just as you would a building block,
or…foundation with a friend.
Then you plant the best of seed
to watch the produce show;
then feed and weed to fill the need
for all good things to grow.

The horse you lead to water there,
but cannot make him drink;
could also be a friend or kin…
or family you link.
Just give them time to reason,
and time enough to thirst,
and when they all are ready,
in line, they'll be the first!

And when in doubt and fear befalls,
and you start to run and hide;
it's fear and doubt that guides you,
and always at your side.
The answer lies in facing
the ills and woe you're bound.
for Jesus Christ the Savior
will help you hold your ground!

The Master Banker

God is in control
of everything we hold;
and heaven is the bank with our account;
we can invest with sound deposits,
or withdraw into the closets;
but the balance on His record shows amount!

So we should place with all our thanks
to the Master of All Banks,
where wealth is not counted as is cash,
but the love that lies within
and the profits that He sends,
makes a higher total there much to stash!

And investments pure as gold
that comes from heart and soul,
and spends a lot of faith in God and man,
is the peace that so arrives,
and the bonds that coincides,
no greater wealth on earth can expand!

And department of the trust
is an absolutely must,
for interest on our earnings to progress;
no credit cards to use to pay delinquent dues,
only prayers and goodness budget best!

So when it's time to go, will your
banking records show...

your statements there are all up to date?
And your debt is paid in full, no credits to annul?
If so, then you're ready for the golden gate!
So the Banker of your life
with His teller, Jesus Christ,
to whom you placed your daily worth,
await with tenderness in heaven's holy bliss,
closing your account while here on earth!

A Cloudy Example

Have you ever stood in the great outdoor
and peered at a cloudy sky?
And see a face you've seen before
in a cloud that formed on high?
Well, I have at times and the cloud defines
exactly who is who;
and the mystery came when the person's name
is someone that I knew!
'Twas a lot of awe and I'd drop my jaw
from facts of the strangest kind,
that no matter in a cloud I saw
was a face that came to mind.

Now, don't deny, simply go and try
on a fleecy cloudy day;
and start by thinking of ole *Abe Lincoln*,
then scan the cloud's array;
I'll swear to you that from the blue,
you'll see his face appear,

with his big bow tie and tall hat too,
and the length of his hairy beard.
I've given this ample, foregone sample,
the next step's up to you;
to test my sample of example
to find my finding true,
that from here on out, you'll have no doubt
of this tale I told to you!

Only in the Fall

It is a fact of life…that God had in His sight;
that everything He did was purposely;
but in His scheme of things…
here's one confusion brings;
and that's the presence of a tree.
Yes, a tree! a gum tree in my yard
and I'm trying very hard
to understand it's certain role.
It's trunk is so profound growing
roots above the ground,
and bustin' up my toes when I stroll.
Then the sticky sap and juices, and
gum balls it produces…
clutters up my yard beneath my boots;
my grass I cannot cut…'til I rake the gum balls up,
but even then there's still the roots!
And I can't cut it down 'cause the
payment would astound,
"an arm and a leg" would be too much;
so I'll live with it I guess, and try to do my best;
while in the yard I'll just use a crutch.
But there's one thing I see…about this gum ball tree,
and that's in the autumn of the year,
when the leaves are brilliant red,
and it's beautiful instead;
"This may be the reason why it's here!"

It Only Takes One Blessing

When evening shadows come to fall
at close of weary days,
just count your many blessings all,
not sorrows or dismays.
For often-times we dwell on woes,
and often we forget;
that even tho' ill winds may blow,
means not our end is met.
For God has given us our gifts,
our lives, for which we owe
our soul to Him for which He lifts
when hard times come to tow.
And every blessing that we count,
even if it's one,
just a simple, honest, small amount,
God sees it as a ton!

Master Mechanic

Our bodies, like cars and old guitars,
all three need a check sometime,
and it takes someone to make 'em all run
by tuning our lives real fine!
But we should inspect the ones whom we check,
to see that we don't get rooked;
so we choose the best to do this test
and not the one who's crooked.
Now if your motor whines and camshaft binds,
then you need a check throughout;
for a tank that boiled or a fuel that soiled,
to find what it's all about!
Now don't show your face down at Satan's place,
'cause he did your work before;
for he's the crook, from your life who took
the strength from your motor's core.
And he's the one who coached it to run,
causing the overheat;
and he burned your wires with his careless fires,
which tangled in a heap.
So upon this time find an ace who's fine
that works with morals pure.
A mechanic fair with a sound repair,
one that will last for sure!
I know of one, the best bar none
with his workplace in the sky:
So, ills or amps that needs revamp,
seek God Who reigns on high!

Hummingbirds

From my window's view I sight
a small hummingbird in flight
to a shrub with flowers bright,
above, a new feeder, a special delight!
She darts past the feeder unaware
this delicious attraction was just hung there;
her eye caught the glare from that liquid of red,
like a bottle of vintage wine rare.

She stops and flutters in her retreat
to sail up and check a newfound treat!
and faster than the sound of her tweet,
she lands on the perch and comes to meet
that wonderful nectar sweeter than sweet.

She flutters and buzzes with great delight,
then away she flew faster than light,
to come again this mighty might,
to her discovery bright.
'Twas only a minute…lo and behold,

there came three more that had been told
by this fluttering, feathered friend in their fold.
They will remain 'til the days grow cold.

I've often wondered how they fare
suspended there in the air,
like a 'copter hovers there,
and where they go, I know not where!
It's all in God's great scheme of things;
to all of us the joy it brings;
to see the hummingbirds come each spring…
to dazzle us with amazing wings!

The Right Temperature

Now I've been thinking and I know it's true;
that is how to manage your marriage through.
There's one thing for certain and two things for sure,
you both stay close as butter to toast…
to work this cure:
First, you agree not to disagree,
then look to see what your spouse there sees;
then decree that you both agree,
then live each day with this appease.

That's number one, but I've only begun,
the next solution is the hardest one;
one needs to listen while your mind is sought;
and don't plan comments while the other one talks.
Hear what is said, then give your reply,
and then you both see eye to eye!

Now last, but not least and the best of all…

is turn down the thermostat that's on your wall.
You turn it back when you go to bed,
this will save your light bill which you dread,
but it does something else you need to know,
it guarantees a closeness for y'all in stow;
for if outside it's cold as ice
with you two cuddled up really nice,
will build a bond when there you clasp;
this will surely make your marriage last!

No Place Like Home

Were you ever in a traffic jam,
and sat there all dismayed?
For the drive you took was just to look—
and home—you wished you'd stayed?
Yes, and here I am hemmed in a van
and can't go to or fro,
'cause up ahead is what I dread,
a parade is on the go!
So, I think of home and should have known
that autos fill the streets;
and often they in awful way
just poke along in creeps.
But, sometimes I, and don't know why,
I just can't sit at home;
'cause of TV, the mess I see,
I find the urge to roam.
So, off I go, to where—don't know;
just have to drive and see;
but now I find I'm in a bind—
with many more like me!
Indeed a mess, now I confess…
(regardless of the strain)
that without a doubt,
when I get out,
I'll never leave home again!

My Getaway

There's a place down by the river,
it's the beauty of the glade;
removed from the noise of daily life;
where I slumber in the shade
mid the marvels God has made,
and everything that's wrong—seems so right!

It's my favorite getaway
where the weeping willows sway,
and the pine trees whisper softly in the breeze;
where the swans and ducklings
graze—
'mid the gentle rippling waves,
beckons me like sailors to the seas.
Where there is no TV noise,
or the violence it deploys,
no motor horns or whistles that I dread;
no telemarket bore who always calls before
you prepare to eat or go to bed.
No blowing leaves next door—
that makes an awful roar,
or wrong-number calls by the phone;
No barking dogs around or any siren sound;
just a perfect spot for me and God alone.

Here, I rest in rapture's might
in pure serene delight,
to guide me along as I pray;
That's why I love this place—
for a little change of pace—
at my quiet and humbled getaway.

PART 5:

HOLIDAY-SEASON POEMS

A Memorial Day Tribute

On the calendar of time
comes a day for all to mind,
in thankful praise with heart and soul;
I'm not referring to a race
that Nascar has in place,
but a tribute to our heroes bold!

For the living, and the fallen,
whom met their duty calling,
every day should bring reminding;
to women and the men, faithful citizens,
a daily "thank you" should be binding!

Nor is it a day
to watch the Yankees play,
or wallow in content upon the beach;
unless, this is to say: "You take the time to pray"
in memory of the Lord and soldiers each!
So let the spirit soar…once again with freedom's roar,
remember 9/11 and those who fell;
"You're with us or you're not"
is the message that I got;
and I hope all the world did as well.
And last but not least, to the living and deceased,
Americans who gave up life or limb,
in the wars that beset, and the challenges they met,
and the light of their glory never dimmed.
So a day is set aside to show our thanks and pride,
to honor all who served us well.
But everyday should be…a call to memory,
so our means and morals never fail!

Another Thankful Day

Well, here we are again, let festivities begin,
Thanksgiving Day has just arrived,
it seems so long a year since our last Thanksgiving here,
"a special thanks to God that we survived."
And though it's just one day to remind us all to pray,
for many folks it's so welcome…I suppose,
for dark clouds daily drift within some people's midst,
which gives no chance to smell that 'verbial rose!

Now God has given us…another chance at trust,
just in case we went astray,
and show to Him in prayer our loyal trust and care,
and do so every single day;
and not just because…it's a holiday to pause,
but for the sake of reason to unfold;
a lifetime undertaking for the
strongest bond in making,
several prayers a year will never hold!
So when we meet to dine leave your politics behind,
leave your worries and your woes at the curb;
the moments that we share is a thankful affair,
"off limits"…to the things that disturb.
Now I sit in my recliner, and nothing could be finer,
aroma from the oven finds my nose,
and from my view I see the leaves all falling free…
filling up the yards in golden rows.

And my wife is in the kitchen, with
the cake she is enriching,
while the water in the kettle comes to boil.
That's for coffee and the tea, and now she's calling me:

"Honey, come take the turkey from the foil!"
Which stops my somber rest to do what I do best,
is carve up a turkey to divide.
The table has been set, preparing has been met,
time for our folks to arrive.
And I hear them coming now, anxious for the chow,
smiling, frisky kids in festive mood;
We assemble with an aim to pray in Jesus's name;
and partake in this gracious food.
So when this day is over, and dark
clouds still may hover,
tomorrow comes the same old way;
it's no different from the rest, life still becomes a test,
just meet them all as you did today!

A Holiday Message

Well, here I am and once again…
July the 4th is here.
It seems this special holiday
rolls swiftly by each year.

I do not need a calendar
to keep up with the times;
because it seems tomorrow brings
those merry Christmas chimes.

It's these two days that come and pass,
what happened to the rest?
Through land and sky they flew on by…
like eagles in their quest.

So just for now I humbly bow,
and wish you all the same:
a happy 4th with peace brought forth
until it comes again!

Happy Birthday, Sister

Happy birthday, Anniebelle,
you sure know how to win!
You showed the world you did it well
through all the thick and thin.
At ninety-six you stayed the course,
and I remember when;
in early days you showed remorse
for someone else's sin.

I love my sisters, seven all,
but you are number one;
always there to catch my fall,
should any stumble come.

And you were like a mom to me
when I was just a lad,
and through the years you came to be
the best friend that I had.

So, carry on, dear Anniebelle,
there's more birthdays in view,
and in our hearts our prayers dwell
for God is loving you!

End of a Busy Day

There's an emptiness that lingers
with our home in disarray,
from little, busy fingers
tearing tinsel foil away!
The smiles upon their faces,
the gleams within their eyes;
their pounding hearts embraces
the secret of each prize.

The shrill of little voices
that filled a gleeful air,
within my heart rejoices
as I view the wrappings there.

But now they have departed,
at close of Christmas Day,
the family we started,
have gone about their way.

The silence that surrounds me;
my lonely thoughts unfold;
brings back my childhood memory
of Christmas Days of old.

Now time is of the essence,
each year our children grow;
our grandkids and their parents
have lives to live, I know.

But another day is coming,
and soon it's New Year's Day,
our heartstrings will be strumming
when they come again our way!

A Warm Reception

It happened on one Christmas Eve,
and one I'll ne'er forget;
while watching news on my TV,
I lit a cigarette;
and on the coffee table stands
an empty whiskey flask,
and I was holding in my hands
an empty drinking glass.
The children all had gone to sleep,
and I stayed up because…
I had to place beneath the tree
the gifts from Santa Claus.
Then there I sat when all was done
and everything complete,
I thought about tomorrow's fun
when all our family meet.
So here was I in restful pose
and puffing cigarettes,
and in my thoughts I closed my eyes
to take a little rest.
Then I suppose I went to dose,
and dropped the cigarette.
It fell into the sofa chair
and fire began to set.
Smoke was rising everywhere
and I began to fret!

Then suddenly a burst of flames
and overhead they flew;
then I saw the fires come down
into the walls they blew.

They leapt and swept and flickered bright
in crimson, gold and red,
and lapped the drapes that once were white,
now blackened rags instead!
And up they soared in violent roar
and spun a vicious core;
and in and out and round about
then back down to the floor.
And up they scooped and down they swooped
the ash and embers there;
with sparks so bright with orange and white,
they set the room aglare.
An' all around a sizzling sound,
as flames came hotter still,
and plumes of smoke joined in the stoke,
to finish off the kill.
Black and charred and badly scarred,
where flames engulfed the scene,
the room was razed in hell-like blaze—
like only hell has seen!

'Twas like I'm glued I could not move,
like mummies as they lie,
and I am caught in dreadful thought:
"Am I about to die?"
For here I choke from all this smoke,
and bound to bid good-bye.
Is this the way I have to pay
for all my worldly sin;
like smoking packs of cigarettes
and drinking wine or gin?
Oh yes, oh yes, it must be true,
my God, what have I done?
To be so rude and careless too,
in what I thought was fun.

"No more dear God," I cried out loud,
"please help me get through this;
for I will nevermore allow
myself to know abyss."

And then I heard a knock and cries:
"Daddy, Daddy, please get up,
the door is locked inside,
we want to get what Santa left
and open up our prize."
Now why on earth would they say that
when smoke or fire is seen?
The truth is—I'd been asleep…
and it's all been just a dream!
When I awoke and realized,
what really could have been,
I prayed to God whom I confide,
I'll not do that again!
But I learned a lesson you can bet,
that it does not pay to drink,
or smoke some nasty cigarette,
that leads you to the brink.
What a day to stop and pray;
let love and goodwill thrive;
on this gorgeous Christmas Day,
It's great to be alive!

Once Upon a White Christmas

I always dreamed of Christmas snow,
a yuletide's pure delight,
but nature only deemed it so…
just one time in my life.
There was a usual atmosphere
that bound our Southern town,
producing fair and balmy air…
when Christmas rolled around.
We rarely ever saw it white,
and never Christmas Day;
that gleaming, brilliant awesome sight
that takes your breath away!
So, I never rolled a ball of snow,
or snowman to enjoy,
or snowball fight with friendly foe
when I was just a boy.

And Santa Claus, while on his round,
I wondered every day:
"How on earth he came to town,
with no snow there upon the ground,
to drive his deer and sleigh?"

Until I heard a song relate,
a "redneck" note it struck;
that Santa used a special freight,
without snow to accumulate,
to drive a pickup truck!
So back into the realm of time,
to one white Christmas Day,
back when I was only nine,
a blizzard came our way.
And I recall that Christmas Eve
when snowfall took its toll,
the town was caught in disbelief
both from the young and old.
We had no fancy sleds to ride
that came from any store,
we were caught in sheer surprise
that never came before.

But there was fun for all us kids,
we had our own device;
we used for slide—old trash-can lids,
and car tires for the ice.
And grown-ups joined in merry fun,
as snowballs filled the air,
and joy came to everyone
in jolly Christmas cheer.
Then Mama made some ice cream snow
as Daddy dressed the tree,
and tied a letter that would show
for Santa Claus to see.
So, therein went my Christmas snow,
when one dream had come true,
and I won't forget that heartfelt glow…
that once came passing through!

In Memory of Mother

When you view the twinkling stars
within the darken skies,
you see the soft reflections there
like shown in mother's eyes.
Always with a gleaming glow
that smiled upon her face;
and everyone adored her so…
with love and warm embrace.

And mother had a zeal for life
without some selfish greed;
she eased the pain of other's plight
by serving those in need.
And she would never let them down,
by faith and serving God,
For she and He were closely bound,
as peas are in a pod!

So herein lies the facts I feel,
that warm me through and through,
for all the strength she came to yield
was courage, brave and true.

For the illness that befell her
in latter days gone by,
purely bore her faith and trust
in mighty God on high.
The emptiness within me,
I'm bound to understand…
that everything is meant to be,

and ends in God's own hands.
And how I love and miss my mom,
now free from ill and pain,
and someday in the great beyond
I'll be with her again!

Easter, a Time to Reckon

Spring is in the air
with blossoms everywhere,
as balmy days of April warms my heart;
it all comes up to mind…
the beauty that I find,
represents our Savior from the start.

Because He sacrificed for us
upon that cross-bound truss…
to free us all from hate, sin, and fear.
And on that fateful day
when our lord was lain away,
little did they know He'd reappear!
For when they moved the stone
they found an empty tomb,
for Jesus Christ our Lord had arose.
Thus, born an Easter Day
when we celebrate and pray,
for miracles in life God bestows!

Every Day Is Easter

On this sunny Easter day
as I bow my head to pray,
a vision comes to mind, and what it means;
I see Jesus hoist on high
upon that cross to die;
stretched and nailed into those wooden beams.

I view Him as he died,
flogged and crucified
as His body hung there, limp and pale;
I can see Him there and now
with the thorns stuck in his brow,
and the blood that trickled down from every nail!

In my sight is Calvary Hill
where the blood of Christ was spilled,
and He died there in a cause for you and me;
If He suffered in this deed
from the sins that all be freed,
can't we endure the pain that comes to be?

When my thoughts go back to see
the scene at Calvary,
the misery that confronts me…disappears.
And my Savior clinging there
with the pain He had to bear,
takes away my troubles and my fears.

For misery seems to fade
by the promises He made,
as joy begins to swell within my breast;

and the love that fills my heart
from my bosom never part,
just trust in Christ and He will do the rest!

So on this Easter Sunday, or any other day,
remember why He died and why He rose;
To save us from our sin;
that souls be born again;
brought about by love that God bestows!

Easter for All

It's apple blossom time, sure and plain.
As the mocking birds are singing in the rain
the bluebirds and the martins find a home.
The squirrels and the rabbits start to roam
and the bees start to build their honeycomb.
It's Easter, but more to explain!
Christmas comes but once a year;
as does Easter, which is here;
so between these two let's not forget;
why Jesus came and why He left;
that every day His word is kept
just to keep our conscience clear!
God brought to us His only Son
to give us strength to overcome;
and believe in Him with all our might,
which brings to us eternal life,
void of all the woe and strife
with all our battles won.

Within my mind I view the scene,
within my heart I feel the sting
of Jesus Christ all limp and pale…
upon a wooden cross is nailed
without a whimper or a wail,
will ever in my bosom…cling!
Good Friday was that day of pain…
when our precious Lord was slain
and laid out in a cavern tomb.
They blocked it with a granite stone,
laughed and cheered the King of Rome,
and thought the end was plain!

But little did the Romans know
what God was holding there in stow,
a miracle that a world would come to bear;
That Jesus braved the blood and pain,
did not die there all in vain,
did not succumb to evil's aim,
but only to arise on Sunday there.
So on this faithful Easter Day
I bow my head and kneel to pray;
thanking God for His love and aid,
the master plan that He laid,
for sacrifices Jesus made…
with all the pain He had to bear!

I Remember Daddy

I sit alone and ponder
while all is quiet and still;
except the ping and splatter
of raindrops on the sill;
except the distant yonder…
yields an echo of a train,
it's whistle, faint and somber
like a sad song in refrain.

The time could not be better,
for the TV's on the blink;
and Grandma took the children
down to the skating rink;
and I sit in my recliner
with a pencil and a pad;
to write a special poem
about my dearest dad;
who long ago in passing
left a memory to behold;
who lived with great compassion
with a heart as pure as gold!

Still, I see my father
as I saw him yesteryear,
as he fought the tribulations
that society came to bear ;
for he was one in millions
who had the grit to stay;
the job of digging ditches
for fifty cents a day!

It took a lot of courage
when depression took its toll;
and Dad was no exception
with eight kids in the fold.
When asked about his worth,
he said: I'm poor as I can be,
but I'm the richest man on earth
for I have my family.

But most of all that I recall
was Dad's true dedication…
to God, to us, to church and all
and daily meditation.
And how he loved a gospel song
when Sunday meeting came;
he would always lead the throng
with all the hymns they sang.

When at last his time drew nigh,
he seemed so reconciled;
he was so weak to even speak,
he just looked at me and smiled.
His victory won at ninety-one,
he raised his arms and cried,
as if to say, "Lord, take me home
for I am satisfied."
And somewhere in the great beyond
I know my father waits,
as does five sisters and my mom…
for me…at the pearly gates!

Another Kind of Christmas

'Tis another Christmas on its way,
I feel it in the air,
It all began Thanksgiving Day…
with bargains everywhere.

Is there a Christmas spirit here
when folks go on their sprees,
to shop around with yuletide cheer
for high-priced Christmas trees?

Or show a smile that Christmas wills
to everyone around,
and show this will with dollar bills…
in discounts that are found?

Just blow away some hard-earned pay…
to find the Christmas groove;
to fill the streets with honks and beeps…
to get someone to move?

To beat the crowd, and shout out loud
in hustle, bustle pace,
to bump and run, to beat the gun…
in Christmas shopping race?

It's not the silver bells that ring…
making the spirit grand,
but constant ring of dough folks bring…
that changes hand to hand!

Now if this shows that I oppose;
"you're mighty right I do"
'cause I resent the money spent…
to make a Christmas true.

So, I'll take my Christmas nice and slow,
which is a better way;
small gifts to go to ones we know…
on Jesus Christ's birthday…
to decorate a small tree bright
that came fresh from the glade,
with little things that flashes light
and things the children made.
And take this special time to share,
to sing, to love and see…
that Christmas time is meant for prayer,
That's what Christmas means to me!

Bright Christmas

Now please don't take me wrong,
but when snowflakes come along,
I love to see their sparklin' glow;
but only coming down
to watch it cover ground…
but guess what? we all become snowbound!

But back in times of old
when winter days were cold
at Christmas time when came the falling snow;
'twas great on Christmas Day
when existed horse and sleigh,
but now in modern times…it just ain't so!

But now we're all snowed in
to our living rooms and den
and can't go out to get our shopping done,
but out upon the street are those whom dare to meet
in a battle of the fittest…barring none.
For all that falling stuff has made it mighty tough;
and Christmas time has turned into a mess;
so trudging in the white…becomes an endless fight,
with everybody's spirit put to test.

So I'll tell you what I'm dreaming,
it's a Christmas that has meaning,
with sunny skies, pretty blue and bright;
when all can skate and run
in usual Christmas fun…
instead of plowing all that snow in sight!

Yes, I'm dreaming of a Christmas
with sunshine in my sight,
and wish your days will also shine;
I'm dreaming of it bright
with the Christmas cards I write,
and without the slippery slopping that we find.
For it hinders us from shopping…
when the snowdrifts deep and blocking
all the cars and people on the roam.
For those who dare attending
and end up "fender bending"
or even slip and breaks a bone;
and probably wished they'd stayed at home!

I'm dreaming of a Christmas,
one when we're out and not tied down,
with our friends we can visit
and everyone will wish it,
a merry Christmas cheer to all around.
I'd be dreaming of a white Christmas,
if we had a horse and sleigh,
like those of long ago…
when there came a Christmas snow,
but in our day and time…there is no way!

So however you may take 'em,
come sunshine, rain, or snow,
you can always surely make 'em right:
just spend the time aglow
for reasons that we know,
and may all your Christmases be bright!

I Remember Mama

Folks could see in Mama's face
as she sang "Amazing Grace,"
when she led the congregation in this song;
a look of sweet content
was the joy that she sent,
for her love for God and church was very strong;
it became her favorite hymn
for it brought her peace within,
but there were others that she loved:
like "What a day that will be,"
"Just a closer walk with Thee,"
"I'll just fly away," and "On the wings of a dove."

The singing made her day,
but her best love was to pray,
and listen to the preachers at the stand;
then came the fond embracing
of the entire congregation,
and if that didn't move you…nothing can!
As a stalwart of the Lord
for whom she so adored,
she practiced what was preached there at home;
with a solid firm belief
as if "set in pure concrete"…
but sweet as a cake of honeycomb.

She lived when times were rough,
to "make ends meet" were tough,
but had the strength to do what e're it took.
to feed ten folks at home
by the source of gardens grown,

and my, oh my, how Mom could cook!
We so lived off the land,
yet it all seemed so grand,
as my thoughts go back to early days of old;
she was always by our side
and always there to guide
when illness in the family would unfold.

And Mom could really sew
just like a tailor pro,
and made up many of our clothes;
and 'mid all the toil that came,
she never once complained,
and why it's true, God only knows.
At the age of ninety-three,
Mama's time had come to leave,
and the Lord claimed an angel for His own;
and I often heard her say:
"I'm longing for the day
when God will work His will
and take me home."

So in 1987 my mother went to heaven,
and there's never any doubt
she earned her way,
now she's in God's warm embrace
with her soft contented face,
which I yearn to see again
some sweet day!

Thanksgiving Day Special

The pumpkins on the meadow side
lie sprinkled fresh with dew;
the falling leaves give graceful glide
as autumn breezes through.
Aroma from the turkey roast
within our nostrils fill,
the pumpkin pie I love the most
is cooling on the sill.
Crispy things that nature brings,
that come this time of year,
from walnut and the pecan tree,
the apple, and the pear,
the "silver queen" and "golden" corn,
and collard greens are there.

Yes, this is a date to celebrate
with joy in festive mood…
thanking God for all we sate
in prayer and precious food.
Though every day we all should pray
with thanks to God above,
but on this special holiday
let's give our special love.
Brought about by sacrifice
with sweat, the toil and tears,
undying faith in Jesus Christ
by early pioneers.
Now, there's so much to be thankful for
on this Thanksgiving Day,
is life and freedom we enjoy
here in the USA.

Born Again on Christmas

Here's a tale told to me
by a friend who's born again.
We sat beneath a church yard tree
with a cool breeze overhead;
with one deep sigh he wiped his eyes,
then this is what he said:
"I stood there all despondent,
downtrodden with concern;
because I lost employment…
from layoffs by the firm.
Three months had passed and counting,
and close to Christmas Day,
my woes were quickly mounting
and my bills I could not pay.
I thought about my children,
Michelle, Darlene, and Wes,
and my wife who had been stricken
with cancer of the breast.
I asked myself this question:
If something does not give,
is life still worth the living
if it comes too hard to live?

Then came my thoughts of others
whom had much wealth abound;
that they will have no problems
when Santa makes his round;
for there'll be gifts aplenty
'mid cheers and joyful bliss,
the children and the grown-ups
will share in happiness.
I wallowed in self-pity, for I could not afford
to buy my family Christmas gifts

because of being poor;
or feel the spirit yuletide brings
when love and cares prevail;
only then to give it up
because the system failed.
And I stood there still and clutching,
(with tearful, swelling eyes,)
the cold and icy railing
that spanned the bridge's rise.
Within my blurry vision…
spume the waters far below,
while making a decision
if time had come to go,
when a voice broke through the stillness
and this is what it said"…
"There's no such thing as illness
if it's only in your head,
for if you die it's certain:
it's not you who bears the woes,
but your lovely wife and children
to solve what life bestows.
It's they who'll bear the burdens,
they, who'll wear the crown
They, whom now are praying
that you will not let them down."
"And when that voice astounded,
I could not tell from where,
but the message that was sounded…
came in so loud and clear.
Was it God's voice conversing?
or an inner voice surreal?
Was it from a passing person
whence came the firm appeal?
But anyway it happened there
I felt a great release,
as if a giant grizzly bear
had swept me to my knees.

Painful tears that flowed before
have turned to tears of joy,
I was stricken by a force of truth
that only God employs.

I slowly rose and almost froze
with chills from bone to bone,
with weakened gait I headed straight
to loved ones left at home.
When I arrived and went inside,
I saw the Christmas tree,
a pine they cut that proved enough
and pretty as could be.
And it was dressed with simple things
like little angels there,
and silver bells that clings and rings
and sparkles 'mid the glare.
And beneath the tree were gifts for me,
like clothes my wife had made,
and photos of the kids I love,
whom asked not what I gave.
My family knew what I went through,
and more than once they said:"
"Daddy, you indeed are all we need,
that nothing else can do;
Christmas comes but once a year,
but we will count that too."

"Back on an icy bridge that night
I think it was a sign,
through snow and rain a voice came
and saved me just in time.
For from that voice there came rejoice,
I laid my burdens down.
I begged the Lord for mercy
and to turn my life around.

And that's the way this story finds…
me blessed in Jesus's name,
for back at that Christmas time,
I was born again."

Thanks for Thanksgiving

In sixteen hundred nine
they sailed the ocean's brine,
in search of a new world for their own;
three hundred eighty-four
are the total years we score,
since the Pilgrims land at Plymouth,
their new home.
In sixteen twenty then,
their new lives would begin;
but many hardships laced their life with pain.
With illness, death about,
their hearts stayed true and stout,
and braved the worst of elements that came.
They struggled hard and long
to keep their purpose strong,
and through it all, good fortune was a friend;
for they met a native tribe
whom they could well confide,
so goals and dreams in life could then begin.
The Indians taught them how
to farm the land and plow,
with other things to guide their way;
they taught them how to tap
the maple trees for sap,
and then the colony was here to stay.
Now because of their success
through all the strain and stress,
they met to celebrate and pray;
giving thanks to God and friends,
that determination wins,
thus, born for us, a good Thanksgiving Day.

Now, just a holiday, it's not…
to lie upon some cot…
and watch a TV game, or dose and nod;
It's a holiday of date,
to pray and celebrate
with family, and friends in name of God;
giving thanks in Jesus's name…
that devoted pilgrims came
for a better life and world in which they paved;
So do not let them down,
for the freedoms that were found…
in Thanksgiving Days…to us they gave.

About Thanksgiving

'Mid the cool and gentle breeze
come Autumn's falling leaves,
which shows Thanksgiving Day is near;
I look forward to it all
when our children come to call;
to celebrate this happy time of year.
There'll be thirteen altogether,
and nothing could be better
as our loved ones gather one more time.
to share our thanks and care
for the reason why we're here,
giving praise to God as we dine.
And the food upon the table
is a symbol and a label,
the first, of course, a turkey roast.
Then there's bread and stuffing mix,
and cranberry sauce real thick,
along with pumpkin pie I love the most.
And I'm sure there'll be some beans
with corn and collard greens,
and sweet potatoes wrapped and baked.
All this precious food
will stimulate our mood,
and for our hungry souls to partake.

And the things we should remember
on this special in November,
is giving thanks to God first of all;
that we're still alive and kicking;
that our lives have not been stricken
by tragic things that could befall.
Then our thoughts and prayers go

to the folks who suffer so,
with loneliness and pain they came to face;
without a single way
to enjoy Thanksgiving Day
with family or friends to embrace.
And last, but not least,
as we gather here to feast,
is pray for our soldiers to survive.
"Protect them, dear God
on the bloody soil they trod,
our faith and trust in You…we confide."
And to all whom fought and died
so our freedoms won't subside,
we dedicate brave honors in their name.
And we shall not forget
the obstacles they met,
like Jesus, they did not die in vain.
So, this Thanksgiving Day
as we give our thanks and pray,
just believe we are the lucky ones;
That it's every day's amount
of blessings that we count,
and not just the holidays that come.

PART 6:

TROUBLED WATERS

A Battle Cry

It's not a war that's fought at sea,
nor land where caissons roll;
not one where guns and cannons roar,
nor bombs that take their toll,
but in the minds and hearts of some…
and the battleground is their soul.
There's been wars and wars,
and rumors of wars,
this one, the greatest fought;
a battle within the bosom of man,
and web in which he's caught.
He tugs each day to find a way
to tread a life he sought.
A war of sin by women and men,
the war zone is their soul;
the games they play with reckless joy…
are played without a goal.
it's nothing new since winds first blew,
a story often told.
And this trend glides like ocean tides
that lap upon its shore;
and on man speeds with thoughtless deeds…
'til he can go no more;
and it will last, 'til lives have passed…
that strayed therein before.
So, how many times must people sin
without a thought of care?
How many times to shun the Lord
and live in doubt and fear?
It's a tough, rough row that all must hoe,
but…they must switch the gear.
To gain the will to bow and kneel,

without any fear or shame;
and ask dear God to come and fill
their hearts in Jesus's name;
to stop deceiving and start believing
that Christ died not in vain.
Still, all the while, others will file
along some sinner's trail,
they too will lose with sex and booze,
and show their lives for sale;
and they'll go on, 'less they atone
from their self-made private hell.
And so, beneath each silent voice
are yearning battle cries;
and there within each burning breast
an inner spirit lies;
so therein marks the battleground…
to win, or face demise.
Now, who am I to say what's best,
or anyone to rate?
Because I knew that wayward path
led to a dismal fate!
and now I feel my life is sealed
by God, and trusting faith.

Only the Lonely

Prologue:
If there are any folks out there
whom show no care or shame;
or to the souls who know despair,
this song is in your name!.

There are concrete prisons in each state
where real crooks do their time,
but other cells where lonesome dwells
are called a "state of mind."
These jails are prisons in some lives
without any walls and bars;
they strangle-hold the lonely souls
who're coping with their scars.
Some are sentenced up to life
with no parole in sight,
and they will stay in their dismay
as victims in their plight.
Where, oh where, are friends who care?
Have they no heart or soul?
Compassion less, and emptiness,
oblivious to console.
It is a world where pains unfurl
in someone's comfort search;
and bitter ends may find no friends,
just others who besmirch.
It's a sad, sad thing when some hearts sting
when pierced by a poisonous word,
but worst of all is hear no call…
with only silence heard.

And the lonely cell is a life of hell…
in jail without a gate;
but the prisoners there have a common share…
they sit alone and wait.
Wait by the wayside lest they find
some inner self-release,
to live by fain, to fight the pain
for everlasting peace.
Peace, ah, peace…what a gracious thing
in a world where folks need love,
where they live on and be unknown,
except to God above.
And someday comes for the lonely ones
when peace will come to all,
for heaven waits for the lone inmates…
who receive their only call.

A Daily Grind

Through the years and through the tears
I've seen the ups and downs;
I fought the force and stayed the course,
and tried to stay in bounds.
But it has been a hectic trend in every daily way,
to meet the call, to fight appall
that comes with every day.
I rise up in the early morn
with planning on my mind,
on how to deal with worldly scorn—
and with the daily grind.
It seems to me—what's come to be—
are people in a rut.
No one agrees, there's no appease,
just different views they strut.
The only answer I can see
is turning to the Lord,
His love and care, His words to bear:
"cease living by the sword"

The Right Tune

I'm weary of the spoils of life.
I'm tired of all the gloom.
Sick of all the talk of strife
and lectures of our doom.
I'm leery of the TV shows
that dwell on woes and crimes,
and all the violence it bestows
upon our children's minds.
I'm disgusted with the media press—
distorting many facts,
just plain angry with the carelessness
of politician's acts.
So, what's the answer to my woe?
The choice comes down to this:
I either stay the status quo
or wave a good-bye kiss.
A better choice I've come to see,
I believe without a doubt,
is tune in just what's good for me
and tune the evil out.

Troubled Hearts

Sometime, somewhere, a body must start,
If they're in some deep trouble within,
To remove the turmoil of a burdened heart
By asking God to forgive them for sin.
Some look to the world and its treasures sought
In hopes of fulfilling their gain,
But they will live on without any thought
Of the cause of their strife and pain.
Their search is ongoing for riches and fame
And yes, some have reached their goals;
But are they aware from whence they came
And the forces that played in their roles?
Is it God that is absent from their heart and mind
As they go through their life of grind?
And is it the Devil's drive in which they find
Themselves in their terrible bind?
But the strain of life is upon us all
And not limited to just the rich,
For many a wealthy one stands tall
By using God's post to hitch.
'Cause God doesn't care how much money we earn
As long as it's honest and clean,
But instilling in us His foundation firm
Is living His precious theme.
So, friends, if you're bothered in any way,
And you're famous and wealthy or poor,
Take all the problems you have each day
And unload 'em at heaven's door;
And the Lord is there to receive them with care,
Which He will dispose at will;
When in heaven we come to greet Him there,
We will have paid Him in full, our bill.

The Right Turn

A crossroad comes in every life
where people choose between:
the proper route that ends their strife,
or way they've always seen.
Now, many reach that crossing road
with dead end straight ahead,
carrying a heavy burden load,
and ill will that was bred.
And many a man has gone astray
with many a wicked deed,
stepped on toes along the way,
and not one heart would bleed.
Some griped a lot in traffic's snare,
and moaned when lights turned red,
smiled not upon a friendly stare,
but cast their frowns instead.
And spatting with their friends—or foe
and yes, their family,
They wonder now which way to go—
to reach tranquility.
So with respect I interject:
you have one choice of two:
that when you reach that intersect—
turn right for life anew.

The Boob Tube

Oftentimes I delved in thought
about our country's moral aim,
and for closure that I sought—
the answer finally came.
While there in my reclining chair,
focused in a TV stare,
suddenly it dawned on me;
that many problems of despair
are fed from that TV.
In olden days when news came slow
by local press and radio;
gave people chance to reason through
in quieter times to bear the news,
to understand if false or true—
instead of TV's present views.
Now, the world news travels fast,
so confused for us to grasp.
For whom we see…all disagree,
too controlled in their broadcast,
just too much for folks like me.
For what we hear compounds our fear
with reckless spin and lies they send
as all the experts drone our ear—
Yes, talk TV will do us in.

A Topsy-Turvy World

The world is turning, but not around,
it's on another course;
the spinning now is upside down
with unrelenting force.
Our country's in tumultuous woe
with wars in every zone,
one is with the terrorist foe,
others here at home.
The politicians fight for votes
in wars that's incomplete,
congressmen are "cutting" throats
of those who seek their seats.
There are soldiers dying every day
in hostile Middle East,
while others in the U S A…
are marching in the streets.
There's something wrong I picture here
with clothing they both wear;
the soldiers with their massive gear
upon their backs to bear;
a heavy rifle in their hands
and heavy boots to tread,
a little Bible in their care…
as death lurks up ahead.
While here are those who sing the blues
protesting with their chants;
in T-shirts and soft tennis shoes,
and usual baggy pants.
The only things they have to fear,
is from some overdose,
or just in case the draft appears,
which changes all their clothes.

What on earth is happening?
I see they're not alone.
The media and the networks
ring demoralizing tones.
There is a saying, and it's right,
about the people's trust;
we cannot win the ones we fight,
'cause enemies are us.
And there is havoc in our schools
where teenage killers roam;
and where the violence overrules
is traced back to their home.
Other wars we're bound to lose
are ones with pedophiles;
they kill our children with abuse,
with jurors in denial.
And where, oh where has justice gone
where crime and drugs prevail?
All these crooks who're living wrong
will serve their time in hell.
Another is with immigrants
whom come to flood our lands,
the terrorist and the Cuban bunch
mix in with Mexicans.
I tell you folks the West is doomed,
as like in suicide;
There'll be no English very soon;
where only Spanish thrive.
Election times, when they appear,
be careful whom you choose,
If we shirk our duty here,
we're all guaranteed to lose.
So what's the answer to all this,
I think God's will is best; I just tell it as it is,
and pray He'll do the rest.

Two Sides to Everything

I may not have to tell you
that our world is in a mess;
for it's saddled through and through
with corruption and unrest.

It's kindled by an awful trend
from whence our woes became;
a surge of hateful crime and sin
that feeds its burning flame!

The world is now a battleground
between the good and bad;
the tools of war or who we are
and where our goals are bound.

The leaders are a choice of two,
The Devil or the Lord;
Jesus Christ, the one to choose,
will do away the sword!

For those whom serve the evil side,
the blood is on their hands,
for they are on a rocky ride
that ends in sinking sands.

'Cause somewhere in the vast beyond,
the good side shall prevail;
and evil ones will then succumb
to backfire's burning hell.

Right On or Left Out

Have you ever been aware
That opinions people share
Just represents confusion everywhere?
There's a lot of "spin" expressed
That adds up to a mess…
Unless we figure out just what is best;
That is…if we need to heed at all
Any notions that befall,
Which show any signs of appall.
For opinions, there are plenty
And everyone has many,
But mostly…none are worth a penny!
And they come from every source
For folks to chart a course,
But given without care or remorse.
For it doesn't take a "brain"
Like that of Einstein's fame,
To see what is right and purely sane;
But…there are telling signs you see
That many are naive,
That everything they hear, they believe.
So you need not be a scholar
To keep from being "hollow."
Common sense applied must surely follow.
No, you need not be an engineer
Or pilot of a Lear;
To understand that words you hear
Must be broad and clear.
And it doesn't take a lawyer's mind
Or doctor you may find,
To figure out what's true in kind
To filter out the grind.
So, when you're watching TV tales,
Or dealing with e-mails,
Common sense always prevails,
And never, never fails.

I'm Just a Bartender

There's a honky-tonk tavern on the edge of town…
with a bar room crowd and the noise is loud;
where the lone souls meet abound.
A small band plays on the center stage
and a crooner whines a song;
how he felt abused and turned to booze
and how his love life all went wrong.

In an atmosphere of smoke and beer
some folks spill the beans…
and I hear their tales of doubt and woe,
and how to manage, they don't know,
and think I should…it seems.

These people come from everywhere
bearing heavy, sad despair,
hoping I can help them cope;
so I listen when I can, and try hard to understand,
but all I can do is hope.
Then I tell them to remember I'm just a mere bartender,
and not the greatest psychic they assume;
but to many I'm a link to save them from the brink…
of falling into the pits of doom.
And I've never seen the like of so many "down the pike"
with all the personal problems that befall;
but I listen quietly with no help that I can give,
'cause I'm not the one on whom to call.
They must take it to the Lord
if they're living by the sword,
if the wish to have their problems cured;
it's the only chance for them to lose their life of sin,

and not depend on me…that's for sure.
'Cause I'm just a mere-bartender
with a shoulder to surrender,
at least to show them I care;
but if they wish to cry it is God they must rely,
for He's the one who answers prayer.

A Human Comedy

There is a "big show" going on,
I've got a front-row seat;
I view the action, hear it's drone
with every sounding beat…
from television in my home,
from out upon the street.
I watch the actors in their play
acting out their theme;
observing how and what they say
and what they really mean.
Sometimes I laugh, sometimes cry,
and times I pine or pout…
because of things that go awry
or how the scenes play out.
The leading actors in this play
are usual folks of fame;
we can see them every day
on TV in their game.
And congress folks who polarize,
no progress have they made;
they're just clowns in mere disguise
with images displayed.
Other actors in this show
are folks like you and me;
standing on the sidelines tho',
we're still in this melee.
The "funny" part about this play
it never seems to end;
the plot continues on each day
with turmoil in it's trend.

Some agree, some disagree,
some take a different view.
The biggest problem that I see…
is seeing nothing new.
And yet, I know what you will say:
"This is the land that's free,
that it's the good old USA with rights to disagree,"
But what I see disturbing me
sings not a pleasant song;
when folks are firm in their decree
and knowing they are wrong.

So goes the show, it must go on…
just play the daily scenes;
the final act is yet to come
with many plots and schemes.
The final act will show the light
when people come to band;
to fill their roles without a fight
and all to understand;
that raising cheers for those who're right,
hurrahs for those who're bound;
will solved the problems of our plight…
and bring the curtain down!

Nowhere to Go——but Up!

I'm on the bottom of the totem pole,
a long way from the top;
it's hard to see a distant goal
with lowest view I got.
I've tried for years to make it up,
but much to no avail;
For long I thought to fill my cup
meant: to pour it from a pail
I've been down a long, long while,
I'm used to all the weight…
which covered me beneath the pile…
that sealed my very fate.
But someone has to bear the load,
it might as well be me;
so any glory down the road
may be my cup of tea.
For in the end I guess I'll win
for I'm their solid base,
for it is me whom folks depend
to hold them up in place.
So when they hand diplomas out
and name the honor role,
my name will be the first they shout
for low man on the pole!

It's Only a Game

There is a trend in sports within,
it's anger people show;
for when their favorites do not win...
they let their tempers go.

I've heard it said that some folks dread
when teams of choice--they lose.
that life itself goes on the shelf...
when their teams get abused.

That it's a dream, a football team
controlling their demands.
from morn to night they scratch and fight
with adversary fans.

They push and shove, shout high above,
and stomp upon the deck;
but when they lose they're in recluse
and come a total wreck.

And in their dens when game begins,
they start to cheer and shout,
but soon the swoon turns into gloom
when things go wrong, they pout.

Then in the street they show defeat
with fist-fights on the ground,
and in the air comes gun smoke there
when someone fired a round.

I heard it's one who shot his son,
because of different view.
Now that's a shame to let some game
come in between those two.
But on it goes, the strife and woes,
too many ills to name;
but why it's so, God only knows,
it's just a simple game.

Two of a Kind

There are two things in this world
that people must resist;
one, are Nile mosquitoes,
and two, are terrorists.
They both have things in common,
which causes much unrest;
their vicious stings which often brings
disruption from these pests!

Both breed in bad conditions
where low life multiplies;
in nests of drear, and far and near,
these pests are on the rise.
The answer is repellant,
a mix that won't dissolve,
like strength of will, a heart that's filled
with power to resolve.

Ben Ruff

King Midas ruled in days of yore,
as legend has it told:
that everything he wished for...
his touch turned them to gold.
Well, he's a distant kin of mine
within my family tree,
but all good fortune he could find,
did not rub off on me!
Because the things I touched in life,
they always turned to naught...
I've known the ins and outs of strife,
misfortunes that I fought.
I hung to pure adversity;
an expert raised on grind;
a hallmark of absurdity;
a sad-sack of all time.
The highway to success became
a rocky trail of woe,
and every time some height I gained,
I fell back down below.
"You see these calloused hands of mine,
that came from wear and tear?
they didn't come from sipping wine
at some high-brow affair."
They grew from climbing cars of coal
by night or day they came;
o'er thirty years of bitter cold,
in heat or torrid rain.
But then I reached my finest goal,
and finally found my place;
I turned to Jesus from the cold
into His warm embrace.

For it was me, the mystery
that I misunderstood;
I never knew how life could be
so sweet and oh so good!
For God had changed my sad outlook
to something fresh and fine;
now through those years the road I took
has vanished into time.

Words to the Wise

Prologue:
"Son, a word to the wise should now suffice…
just go and use your head."
And I heard him good and I understood
those words my daddy said.

So I left his home for a life my own,
but somehow on the way;
the plan I had sorely turned out sad,
but I did learn this to say:
"A genuine plan follows man
until his time is o'er;
and with each one a chance will come
to knock upon his door.
I heard mine knocked, but left it locked
on many a splendid goal.
So here I am like a hornless ram,
with my future still on hold!
And I'm in a net with some regret
for my life is nigh on spent;
but I'll recall some falls I met
and where the efforts went.
Now, if it was great to procrastinate,
I'd come out…way the best;
for first place ribbons by the crate
would on my doorstep rest.
For in the past I saved for last
the many goals I dreamed;
but always went no where fast
in the same old way it seemed.
I loved to hear that auctioneer,
and one I wished to be,

sound off with a voice unclear,
'one dollar, two dollars, three,'
but now I state I chose to wait,
so that did not occur,
and to this day I feel dismay
due to that defer.
I envisioned me upon the sea,
a rugged captain bold;
But just wasn't meant to be
and that plan went to fold.
So I set sails for other trails,
one was a college grad;
but in my sight the funds got tight,
and that dream wasn't had.

Procrastinate? What a debate.
It's the worst ill known to man;
but it's the thing that I do best,
and shows I 'also ran.'
I wound it up as a railroad man,
where thirty years I spent,
almost half a lifetime span
just wondering where it went.
And around my home (I still don't own)
I'm loaded with many a chore;
work my fingers to the bone
going nowhere as before.

So don't be like me, set your will free
and give it all you got;
pursue your goals in high degree
should be your lasting plot;
and don't delay your dreams today
for tomorrow never comes,

reach your height in vigor ways
to better jobs well done.
And after all is said and done,
and your life is fixed by fate,
will your successes add up…none,
because you chose to wait."

A Lost Cause

I was sitting in a chair
in the doctor's lobby there,
when I felt the strangest feeling o'er me creep;
it gripped me like the claws
from a grizzly's mighty paws,
and sent my nerves a-tingling down to my feet!
I came in feeling fine
with no special ills in mind;
just a normal checkup for the year;
but 'mid my deepest thought
of day dreams that I sought,
came the vibrant, ringing pangs that I hear.
I wondered what it was
like a riddle often does,
anxiety seem to cause it all;
and could not point my finger
at the cause that seem to linger,
so I just sat staring at the wall.
Then came a loud and yelling voice,
creating only noise,
and sending crawling tremors down my spine;
no soft or pleasant tune,
but like a knife or spoon
scraping on a sidewalk with a whine.
Then I solved upon my quest…
a reason for the stress,
and (was not the dreaded visit to the docs,)
but an awful screeching sound
like a hound dog in his pound,
howling from a ceiling music box.
You hear them all the time
in restaurants where you dine,

in shopping malls and even in latrines;
they are piped in over air
to lobbies everywhere
to dole out the racket that it brings.
But I found I'm in a trap
when I hear some fellow rap
or a singer calling hogs to stew;
one can't get up and leave,
or mute to be relieved,
one just needs to bear it through.
Now, where on earth has gone
the soft and tender song,
that kept the heart and mind at rest?
they're gone from radios,
TV and music shows,
and I'm sadden by their absence, I confess.

The Ghost Fleet

There's a large amount of names
that the ghost world firmly claims,
and the mystery of it all lingers on;
although those folks exist,
they choose to know abyss,
to live in a place all their own.

Now they could be very shy
as to the reason why,
or maybe it's a dreadful touch of fear;
or could the fact be told
that they're downright inward cold,
and have no heart to really care.

Anyway it goes,
it's only God who knows,
yet…they owe it to themselves;
to fill their verbal cup,
to speak and open up,
to exit all their tight and harden shells.
For there'll be no loyal friends
if they choose to stay boxed in
with a stronger will to hibernate;
It would surely be much better
to connect with just a letter,
before a chance arrives too late.
So, the ghosts that here referred…
with their silence clearly heard,
I hope you soon will see the light;
for on the final page
you'll get a ton of praise…
all you need is—shed those cloaks of white.

A Case of "Rotten" Apples

There are those that dwell among us
whom carry a hidden spot;
that lose the humane trust
that withers into rot.
Like an apple, sweet and rosy
that sparkles unto light,
a sign that oft reposes
'til taking that first bite.
One cannot tell by seeing,
for each cover may deceive,
and so easy to believing
there lies no rotting seed.
Now I've come to know some apples
that wallow in these traits;
but learned resist and grapple,
just toss them in the waste!
It is a must to separate
from apples that are good;
or less the entire apple crate
will die as rotting food.
One person to another;
"Do you have some hidden spot?
A flaw within your cover
to spoil the friends you got?
Do you have that shiny glow
with sincerity at best,
when the truth in saying *no*
is better than a test."
Saying *no* does not bother,
it's the "leading on" that hurts.
especially when some others

fib deep beneath their shirts.
A trend that's seems ongoing,
and I'm hoping it will stop;
prevent the spots from growing
to cease the apple rot.

Down but Not Out

When you're way down in the dumps
and burdened with despair;
can you define the lumps and bumps
of things that got you there?
Are you for sure in certainty
just where to place the blame?
Will you decree for clarity
it's you, you have to name?
'Twas either you or something else
that makes your face so long,
so clean the shelf within yourself
will clear up what went wrong.
One needs to put his life on trial,
his own self be his judge,
and see his style without beguile,
to do away the grudge.
For if indeed someone cast stones
and broke your heart instead…
"it's sticks and stones that break the bones"
and words should never tread.

PART 7:

SEPTEMBER AFFAIR

Engraved in Time

Many years and counting
since our world came tumbling down;
in the form of two trade centers
and the Pentagon renown.
Where scores and scores of people
fell victims to demise,
when Satan's band of heathens
crushed them in surprise.
Forever to remember
the year 2001,
the eleventh of September
will shine for years to come.
For heroes by the thousands
were born upon that day;
their sacrifice with courage,
will in our bosoms stay.
Now once again they're rising
the stalwarts of our time,
the towers of our trademark
and our spirits so entwine.
And we won't forget the terrorist,
who drove this tragedy,
they will bear the scars
that lives in infamy.

Don't Forget to Remember

It's time to remember
The eleventh of September,
To the year 2001;
When a group of Muslim terrorist
Set out to kill and bury us,
Using hijacked airplanes as a bomb.

They flew them into buildings
Which brought about the killings
Of several thousand unsuspecting souls;
And since that time or place
The haven't shown their face,
With the U.S.A. firmly on patrols.

But we've only put a dent
In their effort of intent,
Because the cowards by the millions lie in wait.
They are pacing time to keep,
'Til the minute we're asleep,
Then comes the wrath of bombs they detonate.

The next dates to remember
Were the acts of their agenda,
That led up to the 9/11 affair.
There was pan am 103,
A flight o'er *lockerbie*,
That exploded in mid air;

And that important date came in 1988
December 21, to be exact;
300 lives destroyed, results the cults enjoyed;
With the "scum" who placed a bomb
To impact.

The next to remember is the world's trading center,
Bombed by the terrorist in '93.
This time upon a plan was to use a yellow van,
To match the color of their skin, you see.
And don't forget the bomb they used in *lebanon*,
When U.S. marines were caught asleep in bed.
Was a truck of bombs he drove…In a suicidal mode…
Two hundred forty one were counted dead.
This event occurred…on October 23rd,
In the year of 1983,
It was an early sign what the terrorist had in mind,
To eliminate a free democracy.

There were many other acts, unprovoked attacks,
That came upon our embassies and dwellings.
In Saudi Arabia where *Alqaeda's* mad behavior
Murdered 19 personnel in the service.
It's those barbarous deeds that fill a scoundrel's needs,
and what makes the entire world so nervous.

Now don't forget the *Cole*, a ship they blew a hole,
And killed again our loved ones that we cherished.
But sooner will be better if we all stick together,
The world will rid the evil madmen terrorist.

Undying Embers

Through the air so blue and fair
came horrifying blasts—
that rocked a New York City pair
of structures tall and vast.
Firefighters fought a fiery blaze
to rescue folks in fear,
through all the rage and smoky haze
they also fought back tears.
The sky before—was gleaming bright—
now wroth with smoke and fumes;
that rose above the screams of fright—
in black gigantic plumes;
from towers that had symbol traits;
two monuments in time;
two stalwarts that assimilates
our liberties sublime.
Brought down by men of evil minds—
who targets freedom's choice,
still living in medieval times
with terror in their voice.
Now we shall ne'er forget their act
that stood us all aghast,
but now we're back upon a track
where victory will surpass;
where all the world remembers clear
long after war has past;
'cause justice fans the embers there
still glowing in the ash.

A Ray of Hope

Within our window's lower bay,
a candle cast it's soft-lit ray…
glowing for our soldiers, true and brave;
women and the men,
our children, or a friend,
fighting to remove a terror wave.
Eleven years, and counting,
since their young hearts proud and pounding;
went to battle with a mission fought afar;
they need our hopes and cares,
our utmost sincere prayers,
after all, it's us they're fighting for.
In this raging war on terror,
they are freedom's message bearer;
to silence all the violence in our world.
We never shall abort,
but give our full support
for those whom face the bombings that unfurl.
So, this little flame of lighting
beams a prayer so inviting,
for all our military to come home;
and some will not return,
but their lights will ever burn…
with a special kind of glitter all their own.

9/11 Call

Nine-one-one, 2001,
a quiet and peaceful day;
when no one thought and no one sought:
to see what's on the way.
'Twas Tuesday morn. We were not warned
of shock that lay ahead.
We went about our daily route
in living lives we led.
And in the air in New York there
came forth a grim surprise;
for airplanes engulfed in flames
turned all eyes to the skies.
For evil men committing sin
had crushed our buildings down.
And people fled and people bled
in horror so profound.
When came the surge, Heroes emerged,
and many of them died;
For in that quake, their lives at stake,
the Firemen rushed inside.
It was too late, with too much weight—
the structures soon collapsed;
and many friends and citizens
lay buried in the mass.
They are the brave, true ones who save,
Firefighters and Police;
they, who die in fighting fire,
and those who keep the peace.
And don't forget another jet
hijacked by cunning foe;
flown down upon the Pentagon
and dealt a stunning blow.

Where lives were lost at one high cost,
as smoke plumes filled the air.
And then 'twas known three sites were blown,
and made us all aware.
Then, news arrived that others died
when fourth plane crashed below;
because brave men who fought within
had overthrown the foe.
And you can bet the terrorist threat
had sights on Washington;
and to those men who hog-tied them,
our gratitude they won.
With broken hearts and tears that start,
we swore we shall unite;
we made it clear we have no fear,
and now it's time to fight.
Just as you read, the missiles speed;
the war has just begun,
and it won't stop until they pop
and justice shall be done.

A Solution for Pests

They live like bats and moles
in their dirty caves and holes,
emerging only if the "coast is clear"—
to terrify and kill
and destroy people's will,
aiming to create doubt and fear.
They rule *Afghanistan* by the name of *Taliban*,
rodents in disguise as shapes of men.
They harbor and support
the cowards in their fort,
but the pesticide of freedom does them in.
In a recent coward act
when our country was attacked,
their aim was to shower us with fright.
It brought us to our knees…
but not for them to please,
but with every heart to pray and unite
The terrorist only thought
the outcome which they sought,
would terrorize the USA—
but it backfired in their face,
the plan they had in place,
and the cunning force of evil will now pay!
Now they may hit their marks
and cause a lot of sparks,
but never will they dent our souls;
our courage shall prevail,
and our mission will not fail,
we'll put them underground
back with the moles.

A Wake-Up Call

Not since nineteen forty-one
has a deed like this been done,
a horrifying act upon our land;
when the lowest of the low
dealt us a stunning blow,
with airplanes as bombs they had at hand.
They are cowards on the prey—
who sneak in night or day,
to interrupt our freedom we hold dear.
They may crush our buildings high,
but our spirit will not die,
they'll hear our patriotism loud and clear.
Over bodies that have bled
were many tear drops shed,
our country now is rising to the test.
We hold our freedom strong
and when evil comes along,
our courage and our strength
are at their best.
But because our trust ran deep,
we were caught here while in sleep,
but it doesn't mean we're not defiant…
nor ever on the take,
which was their inept mistake,
for what they did was wake a sleeping giant.
So let it now be heard,
the ring of every word:
"America is here to stay.
We're united, everyone…
and our mission will be won,
and God will Bless the USA."

The Rock

In this day and time
with our freedom on the line,
we need a solid footing which to stand;
we must not slip and slide
when tragedies arrive,
but band together all—hand in hand.
For binding oft' installs
strong bridges, and not walls!
Thus, the greatest force on earth
can't be denied.
We need not show alarm
when evil does us harm,
because the Rock of courage
is our guide.
For the greatest force on earth
is a power, given birth,
when the voices of the people rise as one,
and in the face of war
we can come just as we are,
and the enemy of goodness shall succumb.
For the leader on our side,
and the one whom we abide,
is Jesus Christ our Savior, Son of God.
He is the Rock within our soul,
who masters our stronghold,
to cast away the evil of Jihad.
So lean onto the Rock,
the key is to unlock,
and open up the gates that harbor fear,
and the Lord is there with care
to comfort our despair,
and bring about the peace we hold so dear.

Now Is the Hour

We need each other more and more,
we dare not shrink or cower;
There comes a call like none before
that rings "now is the hour!"
For all of us are warriors now;
our duties are the same,
'twill take the sweat from every brow
for enemies to tame.
We need not fire a single shot,
nor yield a bayonet;
but show the foe that we are not
the weaklings they beset.
We must unite in this new fight—
against such different foes;
who are unknown and freely roam
right here beneath our nose.
We pledge allegiance to our cause;
to country and to God;
and be alert without due pause—
so evil will not trod.
We all must work, together perk
with loyalty and pride;
forget the fears and dry the tears,
and stand for those who died.
We are at war, an unknown war
that changed both young and old;
for nothing in our lives so far
has taken such a toll.
But if we show our real true grit,
and nevermore give up;
even if it's bit by bit
will fill our freedom's cup.

Stand resolute in strength and will
with our undaunted power;
'til comes the day peace is fulfilled—
will be our finest hour!

Always Remember

Battle 1, we may have won,
but much work still remains;
the war's not done—it's just begun,
too early to make claims.
It's easy now to lose the sight
of horror that was spread,
arousing us from sleeping tight—
to wide awake instead!
So, as we move along in time,
never should we forget—
the image fine they left behind,
each sacrifice they met.
The praise of those true-brave heroes
will ride upon the wind.
and on it blows 'til it bestows
a peaceful, lasting end.
Then cast our missiles not astray,
nor store our cluster bombs,
but blast away with every day
until our victory comes!

Four Sites of Fire

The world will long remember
four sites of agony;
from eleventh of September—
into eternity.
The mission came from terror groups;
to hijack and to kill;
destroy all our freedom roots
and break down our goodwill.
One target was the Pentagon,
our military home,
where from the blue an airplane flew
and crashed in as a bomb.
And targets were the towers tall
that rose in New York skies,
but those two giants began to fall—
when blown into demise.
The shock was devastating,
the scene was so surreal,
then came the news relating
to a Pennsylvania field.
Where crashed another aeroplane
when brave men overthrew—
the madmen whom had evil aim
to kill the entire crew.
And heroes born aplenty
within that tragic day;
for at those sites rose many
with their courage on display.
And to these sites we'll cherish;
they'll live in infamy,
that it be known to terrorist—
they can't disturb the free!

Ground Zero

There's a site in New York City
we all have come to know;
'twas torn with plight and pity
so they named it Ground Zero!
Where vapors from the aftermath
still streaming skyward bound;
reminding us of Satan's wrath
that fell those structures down.
Where every day in God's embrace
come angels from the slain;
instills an image of that place
where memory will not wane.
As "dust to dust" is often said—
this case is, oh, so true!
For many people that are dead—
were never found in view.
But always in the vast beyond
their spirits ever soar;
o'er the walls that rise anon—
to shine there as before!

Heroes All

There's a group of men and women
we may never know at all,
they may never get attention
with a plaque upon their wall,
but in our hearts forever
as we look upon the past,
their fearless self-endeavor
will in our bosom last!
We always shall remember
those heroes on that day,
the eleventh of September
when their lives were all at bay.
And also all the others,
the victims caught inside;
mothers, sisters, brothers,
dads and sons who died.
And as we wave *"Old Glory"*
let's pay tribute to them all;
for time will tell the story—
how brave souls met their call.

The Last Phase

Gone the structures once gigantic;
Oblivion's pantry claims them all.
Fallen walls that silenced panic,
There lay heroes 'neath their pall.
Remnants laid by havoc's spree…
Now, 'mid damp and cold—men toil,
Gentle hands seek tenderly,
Sifting, lifting through the soil…
They seek remains of loved one's ending,
God alone has found their souls.
All the heartaches will be mending—
When the plan of God unfolds.
Lift us all to God's own Castle;
There our loved one's wait above,
Leave behind the woes of hustle—
Rapture in God's own true love!